York's Hidden Stories

Rachel Wicaksono • Dasha Zhurauskaya

York's Hidden Stories

Interviews in Applied Linguistics

Rachel Wicaksono
School of Education, Language and
Psychology
York St John University
York, UK

Dasha Zhurauskaya
Independent Scholar
York, UK

ISBN 978-1-137-55838-1 ISBN 978-1-137-55839-8 (eBook)
https://doi.org/10.1057/978-1-137-55839-8

This Palgrave Pivot imprint is published by the registered company Springer Nature Limited.
The registered company address is: The Campus, 4 Crinan Street, London, N1 9XW, United Kingdom

In memory of JZ

PREFACE

York's Hidden Stories: Interviews in Applied Linguistics presents a case study of an applied linguistic project from conception to completion. The book provides a unique resource for students, academic researchers and project leaders who are interested in using interviews as a method of data collection for their research project. Experiences of migration have probably always been, and continue to be, some of the most common and yet important and difficult stories to tell/hear. This book explores the making of migration stories that were elicited as part of a community project in York, UK, and makes recommendations for project leaders and researchers who are planning to use interviews in a community project.

WHY (HIDDEN) STORIES?

Everyone tells stories about themselves, their friends, enemies, people they have met and even people they have never met but feel like they know. These narratives might be elaborate and regularly told or they might be small snippets of mundane information, embedded in everyday conversation. In its various forms, 'narrative is international, transhistorical, transcultural: it is simply there, like life itself' (Barthes 1977: 79).

Getting people to tell their own stories is a technique that historians (have) use(d) 'to tell the history of ordinary people and to explore what life was like for them, on their own terms' (Merrill and West 2009: 18). 'Ordinary people' probably means non-Kings/Queens/Presidents in this context. It hardly needs pointing out that *everyone* (including royalty and politicians) is both 'ordinary' *and* 'not ordinary', depending on where they are, what they are doing and who is judging their 'ordinariness'. The meaning of ordinariness is inextricably embedded in the context within which it exists and, as such, functions to restrict and enable interaction between individuals and institutions. Stories have the potential to demonstrate how the meaning of '(not) ordinary' gets made and how, once accepted for what they 'are', these meanings affect the lives of the storytellers and the audiences for their stories.

The community project we describe in this book was designed to elicit stories that were considered by the project leaders to be 'extra' ordinary, so ordinary that they were unnoticed, ignored and thought (by residents) to be of no relevance to the city in which the storytellers were currently living. The aim of the project, which we describe in more detail in Chap. 2, was to unhide the migration stories of residents born outside of the UK and to challenge those residents who might think of themselves as having a greater claim on the city of York than the more recently arrived. In this way, the project hoped to contribute towards the building of an alternative history of the city, one that is knowledgeable about, and accepting of, all its residents.

Given that the meaning of '(extra)ordinary' stories is embedded in the contexts in which they get told, the final meanings of these (and any) stories are destined to remain 'hidden'. This doesn't mean, we believe, that the stories told here, or any stories, are pointless, rather the opposite: for stories to have meaning, they need to be constantly told and heard. Hidden and (un)hiding stories are complex states/processes, and we come back to them in more detail in Chap. 2 of this book.

WHO IS THIS BOOK FOR?

This book is written for researchers and community activists, and anyone who is, or wants to be, either or both of these. The book suggests reasons for, and ways in which, interviews can be used to learn more about the lives of the people around us, giving people power over the presentation and meaning of their experiences. For anyone interested specifically in the experience of migration, there are stories told here that shed light on this most important (and yet extra-ordinary) topic of our time.

How Is This Book Organised?

The book is divided into five chapters. Chapter 1 begins with an overview of a range of possible reasons for the use of interviews as a research instrument and then explores several possible ways of analysing interview data. The second half of Chap. 1 explores the disciplinary context of the case study, applied linguistics, and comments on the extent to which various approaches to interviewing meet the 'requirements' of the discipline.

In Chap. 2, we present a number of community-based projects that have used interviews to discover stories, including our case study: York's Hidden Stories. In reporting on this project, we aim to provide a 'real-world' illustration of some different approaches to interviews as research data, as well as how these approaches might work for applied linguists.

Chapter 3 provides a detailed description of the interview data we collected and analysed for our case study. It covers the two very different methods that we used in the analysis of the data and the theoretical frameworks that underpin these methods. The ethical challenges of the study are explored at the end of Chap. 3.

Chapter 4 includes analysis of the case study data, a discussion of our findings and a set of recommendations following the analysis. This chapter is organised into two sections to reflect the two different methods of data analysis used in the case study.

Finally, Chap. 5 draws conclusions and discusses the limitations of the case study. We also, as applied linguists, outline a set of recommendations for the use and conduct of interviews as part of community projects where the discovery of hidden stories is an aim.

How Can This Book Be Used?

Readers interested in the stories of the participants in our project will find Chap. 4 the most interesting and the best place to start reading. For community project leaders, or anyone thinking about using interviews to create and present experiences, Chaps. 2 and 5 have some practical suggestions. Chapters 1 and 3 are most likely to be of use to (student) researchers who are in the process of deciding whether interviews might help them meet their research aims and, if so, how they might collect and analyse their interview data.

Who Are the Authors?

Dasha Zhurauskaya studied English language and linguistics at York St John University at undergraduate level and has a Master's by Research from the University of Leeds. Dasha was born in Svetlogorsk, Belarus, and lives in York. Rachel Wicaksono is a graduate of the Universities of Oxford and London (Institute of Education). She is Associate Professor and Head of the School of Education, Language and Psychology at York St John University. Rachel was born in County Durham in the North of England and, after many years overseas, now also lives in York.

York, UK   Rachel Wicaksono
                                                  Dasha Zhurauskaya

References

Barthes, R. (1966/1977). Introduction to the structural analysis of narratives. In R. Barthes (Ed.), *Image-music-text* (S. Heath, Trans.). Glasgow: Collins.

Merrill, B., & West, L. (2009). *Using biographical methods in social research.* London: Sage.

ACKNOWLEDGEMENTS

The authors would like to thank the Centre for Global Education, in particular its project leaders, for allowing us to use the York's Hidden Stories data. Thank you also to the participants in the project who consented to the inclusion of their stories in our study.

Without the assistance of our three student researchers, funded by the York St John University 'Students as Researchers' scheme and the HEA National Teaching Fellowship fund, we would probably still be at the stage of transcribing our interview data. So, thank you to Aroob Qaimkhani, Jade Bassindale and Harriet Palmann (and congratulations on your First Class Honours degrees in English Language and Linguistics).

We are very grateful to the anonymous reviewers of our manuscript, and their excellent suggestions for the content and structure of this book.

For useful feedback on our study at a critical point in its development, we would like to thank Professor Fiona Copland of Stirling University and Professor Bob Garvey (then) of York St John University.

Finally, we are extremely thankful to all our current and former colleagues at York St John University, especially Professor Christopher J. Hall, Professor Helen Sauntson and Dr Andrew John Merrison. This book would not have been possible without their intellectual contribution and collegial support.

CONTENTS

CHAPTER 1

Interviews: Perspectives from Applied Linguistics

Abstract This chapter offers an overview of possible uses of interviews in applied linguistics. It begins by suggesting some reasons for the prevalence of interviews in our daily lives and for their popularity as a research instrument. The chapter explores a range of different theoretical perspectives on the collection and use of interview data. Focusing on the disciplinary context of applied linguistics, this chapter comments on the extent to which various approaches to interviewing meet the 'requirements' of the discipline.

Keywords Interviews • Applied linguistics • Neo-positivist • Romantic • Constructionist • Transformative

This chapter begins with a review of reasons for the use of interviews and some ways of analysing interview data. The second half of the chapter explores the disciplinary context in which we are working, applied linguistics, and comments on the extent to which various approaches to interviewing meet the 'requirements' of our discipline.

© The Author(s) 2020
R. Wicaksono, D. Zhurauskaya, *York's Hidden Stories*,
https://doi.org/10.1057/978-1-137-55839-8_1

Why Interview?

Turn on the television, tune in to the radio or go online, and it is clear that interviews are a very important form of interaction in everyday life. As Atkinson and Silverman (1997: 304) have noted, we live in an 'interview society'. Perhaps it is this familiarity with the genre that makes interviews such a common way for researchers to interact with their participants and 'still the most preferred form of qualitative data' (Silverman 2004: iii). But interviews are not only familiar, they are also often felt by researchers to be useful, flexible and easy to do (Talmy 2010). We could add that they are likely to be interesting, even fun, to do when the topic of the interview and the participants are chosen by the researcher, as they usually are.

So, as a way of collecting research data, interviews do not require any explaining or justifying to potential participants, who are very likely to already know exactly what is expected of them. However, this very familiarity with the idea of the interview is also a potential drawback of their use as a research instrument. Because we are surrounded by interviews, we are also desensitised to their form: structure, language, expectations, roles and so on (Mann 2011). Interviews, in other words, are part of the research furniture and, as such, could potentially be no longer noticeable or of interest. Fortunately however, the popularity of interviews in academic life is also reflected by the fact that their use, both as a method of data collection and a methodology, has become a topic of research in itself (e.g. Cicourel 1964; Kvale 2007; Talmy and Richards 2010; Roulston 2010; Talmy 2010, 2011; Roulston 2011; Mann 2016). Not allowing the interview to become just part of the research furniture, these scholars, and others, have, in ways that will be explored later in this chapter, re-sensitised us to the interview and its workings in and on our research.

In the next part of this section, we consider a range of different ways of thinking about interviews and how these different conceptualisations of the genre might influence a researcher's reasons for interviewing. We have already noted how frequently interviews are to be found in everyday life and in academic research; they are generally thought to be useful, flexible, easy to organise and fun. Underpinning the idea that interviews are 'useful' are a wide range of assumptions about the 'content' they generate and the way in which this content gets generated, the role of the interviewer and other aspects of the interview (e.g. place and recording equipment), and the status of the interviewee as a person that can be separated both from the interviewer and from the context in which the interview takes place. Of the many possible ways of thinking about interviews, we have selected four to look at in some detail, and we very briefly mention a number of others for readers who may be interested in exploring these. The four conceptualisations we explore here are neo-positivist, romantic, constructionist and transformative. We have chosen these four because they are also the focus of a special issue of *Applied Linguistics* (Volume 32, Issue 1, 2011) that remains an important marker in the development of interview research in applied linguistics. In the next chapter of this book, we show how these four ways of thinking about interviews played out in the analysis of the interview data collected for the community project that forms the case study presented here. The brief mention of other approaches aims to point at potential future directions for interview research.

If interviews are 'obviously' useful, flexible, easy to do and (maybe) fun, why should we (community activists or academic researchers) bother to think in any further detail about why we are using them to do our work? Methods of data collection and analysis have themselves become topics for discussion in the research literature, with users explaining what their preferred methods can be used to achieve and advising other users not to be inconsistent (e.g. Talmy 2010) or to misunderstand or confuse methods and the reasons for their use (e.g. Braun and Clarke 2019). In participating in the community project that we present here, we noticed that our own reasons for doing interviews (and therefore our understanding of the meaning and possible uses of interview data) were different from (what we understood of) the project leaders', and maybe the participants', reasons and understandings. These differences seemed like more than just different beliefs about the same 'thing' but like beliefs about different things. Thinking about these things became part of our study. We say more about why they did in the section below on the disciplinary context of our study. As we say above, the four conceptualisations we explore in this chapter are neo-positivist, romantic, constructionist and transformative. We begin with the first two, both underpinned by the idea of the interview as a research instrument (Talmy 2010).

Neo-positivist reasons for choosing to interview are related to the assumption that interviews are an effective way of generating detailed accounts of events or thorough descriptions/explanations of beliefs and actions. Where the purpose of an interview is to uncover an accurate and detailed account, the interviewer is likely to consider themselves a neutral figure who, through careful preparation, aims to ask 'good' questions which reduce, or remove, bias in their findings. In this way, it is assumed, the interviewer produces good quality data that, in its straightforward relationship to the questions asked, is 'valid'. According to Briggs (2007: 555), researchers working in this tradition commonly portray interviews as carefully structured to 'elicit inner worlds with minimal intervention'. This approach to interviewing is one which seeks to 'mine the attitudes, beliefs and experiences of self-disclosing respondents' (Talmy and Richards 2010) who have been made to 'forget about the [interview] event so that interviewers can access their "natural" behaviour' (De Fina and Perrino 2011: 1). Interview responses are thus assumed to be, and presented as, direct representations of people's thoughts and experiences (Silverman 2013). This rationale for interviews has been described as 'you ask they answer, and then you know' (Hollway 2005: 312).

Another version of these beliefs is that interviews are thought to be/ presented as a way of generating 'true confessions', self-revelations about thoughts, actions, and attitudes to events, which would not be possible without the empathetic skill of the interviewer. Where the interviewer aims to access 'true confessions', they are required to actively establish a positive rapport with the interviewee, allowing for an intimate conversation that provides insight into the authentic life-world of the interviewee. In contrast, establishing such a relationship is not likely to be part of the practice of interviews that are conducted for the reasons described in the previous paragraph. Those interviewers who aim to elicit detailed and accurate accounts are more likely to try *not* to create any kind of relationship with their interviewees, in the belief that a lack of neutrality could introduce bias into their data and undermine the validity of their findings. In a taxonomy of uses for and beliefs about interviews, Roulston (2010: 51) categorises interviews that are undertaken for 'neutral' reasons as 'neo-positivist' and interviews undertaken for confessional reasons as 'romantic'. Both neutral and confessional reasons for interviewing are 'naturalistic' (Silverman 2004: iii) in the sense that the interviewers aim to document in detail the 'real' world of the interviewees in ways that, for example, questionnaires (lack of detail/depth) and observations (no access to the thinking of the participants) cannot.

In contrast to these neo-positivist/romantic ways of thinking about interviews, a constructionist perspective treats the interview as a socially situated 'speech event' (Talmy and Richards 2010: 2) which actively shapes the participation of both interviewer and interviewee. This is an orientation to interviewing which understands interviews not as a 'neutral' research instrument but as a form of 'social practice'. Constructionist conceptualisations of interviews recognise the interactional context of the interviewee's responses and treat these not as direct representations of the interviewee's thoughts and experiences but as 'situated accountings' (Roulston 2010: 62). Holstein and Gubrium (2000, 2004) similarly suggest that interviews should always be thought of as active meaning-making ventures in which it is not possible to divide the interviewer's input and the participant's interpretations. As Mann (2011: 6) says, 'all interviews are already sites of social interaction, where ideas, facts, views, details, and stories are collaboratively produced by interviewee and interviewer'. On interview questions, Clark and Schober say the following:

> It is futile to search for truly neutral questions. They don't exist. Every question carries presuppositions, so every question establishes a perspective. So for each question we must ask: Is the perspective taken really the one from which we want the respondent to answer? If the answer is yes—if we can justify the perspective—then we can also justify the question. (Clark and Schober 1992: 30)

In summary, a constructionist approach assumes that interviews do not stand for anything other than themselves and that interview data can only tell us about how the participants 'do' interviewing at the time of their interaction. A constructionist approach, however, does allow us to observe the mechanics of how actual life stories get made and distributed and, if we wish, to speculate on the possible consequences of these life stories for the interviewees.

We have presented three main ways of thinking about interviews: neo-positivist, romantic and constructionist. After Roulston (2010), we are calling our fourth and final category 'transformative'. Transformative conceptualisations of interviews take as a starting point the belief that neo-positivist/romantic (and perhaps some constructionist) approaches fail to pay sufficient attention to the complexities of our gendered, socially and ethnically stratified world and of our own thinking and writing. Highlighting the form of the word itself, Schostak says:

> The inter-view maps what is at stake in the multiplicity of views that create the everyday fields of struggle. [...] What is worth fighting for, arguing for, building, emerges through the inter-view, the dialogue of the views of peo-

ple who seek recognition and representation of their differences. (Schostak 2006: 178)

From a transformative perspective, the act of interviewing is underpinned by an awareness of the complex relationship between interviewer and interviewee. The participants in the act work jointly to develop new understandings of their experiences and challenge normative interpretations. The participants may also aim to use their interview data and any discussion of their findings to benefit the interviewees, by raising awareness of aspects of their lives or challenging interpretations of their experience in order to change public attitudes and, perhaps, government policy or law. Marn and Wolgemuth (2017: 365) sum up this approach to interviews as follows, 'transformative interviewers assume that all human interaction is interventional in some way and therefore seek to conduct interviews to intervene with intention'.

So far, we have considered four ways of thinking about interviews (neopositivist, romantic, constructionist and transformative) and how these different conceptualisations of the genre might influence a researcher's reasons for interviewing. In Chap. 2, we exemplify a number of these ways of thinking about interviews with reference to our case study. In the next section of this chapter, we consider some ways of interviewing and analysing interview data.

Finally, in this section, we briefly point to two other ways of thinking about the use of interviews, both of which are extensions of a transformative approach. The first way uses interviews to achieve de-colonising aims (e.g. avoiding using terms that are not relevant or welcomed by the participants, not claiming knowledge about 'others', and providing space for participants to reflect on and use their peers' accounts of their experiences) (see, e.g. Bartlett et al. 2007). The second way draws on new materialist ideas about the relationships between the interviewee's contribution and the material aspects of the situation in which the interview takes place (including interviewer, recording devices, place, time, assumptions about possible audiences). We come back to these 'new' ways in Chap. 5, when we speculate on possible ways out of the (binary) categorisation of interviews as either research instruments or interviews as social practice.

How to Interview?

At the time of writing this chapter, an internet search using the words 'how to interview' resulted in 1,160,000,000 results. The vast majority of the advice available online concerned job interviews: how to conduct job interviews effectively (including how to avoid illegal or inappropriate questions) and how to get the job you want by performing well in job interviews. Some of the advice was aimed at (aspiring) journalists, interested in the types of broadcast interviews we mentioned at the beginning of this chapter: eyewitness, celebrity, opinion and so on. More information on the topic of journalist interviewing can be found at BBC Academy webpages, which provide a range of useful resources from experienced interviewers (BBC Academy 2019). Amongst the advice to be found in the first fifty pages of the internet search results was how to interview if you need to choose a roommate, investment advisor, plastic surgeon, architect, nanny, counsellor, psychologist, psychotherapist, estate agent, caterer, property manager or divorce lawyer.

Advice was also available in these first fifty pages on interviewing a range of participants, including survivors of sexual and gender-based violence, immigrants (when you don't speak their language), your own parents, politicians, cosplayers, musicians and your heroes. There is also advice online about interviewing to elicit life stories, including the East Midlands Oral History Archive 'How do I conduct an oral history interview?' (n.d.), the Veterans History Project 'Sample interview questions' (2005), the Oral History Project: Giving Voice to the American Latino Experience 'How to video' (2015) and Bangla Stories 'Interviewing your own family' and 'Recording memories (technical help)' (n.d.).

Any university library with a research methods section is very likely to have several textbooks that include advice on how to interview (see, e.g. Brinkmann 2018; Brinkmann and Kvale 2015; Gubrium et al. 2012; Kvale 2007; Rubin and Rubin 2012; Seidman 2012; Silverman 2010, 2013, 2015). There is an up-to-date list of recommended reading about interviews on *Qualitative Interviews* (2020), a website maintained by Steve Mann of the Centre for Applied Linguistics, University of Warwick, UK, that lists books, journal articles and web-based resources about interviews.

In the context of all this advice, the aim of our case study presented in this book was to see whether we were able to make any recommendations for 'life story' interviewers from the perspective of applied linguistics. Our suggestions are presented in Chap. 5 of this book.

Analysing Interview Data

How a researcher decides to analyse their interview data should be related to their reasons for conducting the interview in the first place. In this section, we briefly describe methods of/approaches to the analysis of interview data that are consistent with the four categories we identified above: neo-positivist, romantic, constructionist and transformative. These approaches to analysing interview data are as follows: thematic analysis, narrative analysis, critical discourse analysis and (applied) conversation analysis.

Thematic Analysis

Thematic analysis is a common way of analysing qualitative data by noticing patterns within the data in order to report what seem to the analyst to be the main issues that are dealt with in the data set (see, e.g. Attride-Stirling 2001; Boyatzis 1998; Braun and Clarke 2006; Gibbs 2007; Tuckett 2005). The first stage of thematic analysis is usually to code, for example, an interview transcript for important words, phrases or ideas. Boyatzis (1998: 63) defines these words, phrases or ideas as 'the most basic segment, or element, of raw data or information that can be assessed in a meaningful way regarding the phenomenon'. These elements are then grouped into larger categories, and the relationship between the elements within the categories, and the categories themselves, is explored. In the presentation of the findings of a thematic analysis, extracts from the data may be used to usefully exemplify the categories of which they form a part. Mann (2011: 2), however, cautions that these selected voices, though 'appealing, varied and often colourful [...] tend to be presented bereft of context and methodological detail'. Braun and Clarke (2006, 2019) emphasise the importance for researchers choosing to use thematic analysis to clearly outline their theoretical and conceptual frameworks in order to avoid confusions between (what they think of as) distinctly different approaches to thematic analysis.

More information about how we used what our 'clients', the York's Hidden Stories project leaders, described as thematic analysis, and the benefits and drawbacks of our response to their request for this type of analysis, can be found in Chap. 3 of this book. In the next section of this chapter, we say more about the issue of 'client' in our disciplinary context, applied linguistics. In Chap. 5, we return to the issue of working with clients who are outside our institutional context, the university, and make some general comments about the benefits and challenges of public engagement.

Narrative Analysis

Early narrative analysis (e.g. Labov and Waletzky 1967, also using interview data) focused on narratives as highly organised structures with a beginning, a middle and an end. The Labovian approach to analysis positioned the interviewee as the producer of their own story and its meaning. Later versions of narrative analysis were 'identity focused approaches related to the narrative turn' (De Fina and Georgakopoulou 2008: 380) that were based on social interactional/constructionist perspectives. In other words, the belief that oral narratives, regardless of the context they appear in, should be seen as talk-in-interaction. A perspective on the notion of talk-in-interaction is discussed in more detail in relation to conversation analysis, below.

Critical Discourse Analysis

Critical approaches to research (see Fairclough and Wodak 1997, for a useful typology) aim to detect and unmask beliefs and practices,

> that maintain the status quo by restricting the access of groups to the means of gaining knowledge and the raising of consciousness or awareness about the material conditions that oppress or restrict them. (Usher 1996: 22)

Critical discourse analysts reject the assumption that the production of texts is separable from the contexts in which they are produced. Critical discourse analysts pay attention to the social location of speakers and to how the talk that they produce is always influenced by a social interest, in other words, the social construction of meaning/understanding (Usher 1996).

The social location of interviewers and interviewees can include: their status as questioners/project workers or questioned/beneficiaries of the project, their social status in their current context (see Rodger and Herbert 2007), their prior relationship (Garton and Copland 2010), their perceptions/expectations of the interview genre and their access to the language in which the interview is conducted. However, rather than taking for

granted the nature of the relationships between discourse and social location (including beliefs, objects, people and relationships), critical discourse
analysts look in detail at the role of texts in how beliefs about the social
world and physical world come about, how beliefs change over time and
between places, who is advantaged or disadvantaged by which kinds of
texts (and talk) and how any disadvantage could be avoided or corrected.
These concerns echo those whose perspective on interviews can be
described as 'transformative' (see the previous section on 'Why Interview?').

(Applied) Conversation Analysis

The origins of conversation analysis lie in the works of Garfinkel (1967)
and Goffman (1983) on the social order and the complex organisation of
everyday human interactions, and in subsequent work by Sacks, Schegloff
and Jefferson (ten Have 2007) on patterns of talk in interaction. Initially,
much conversation analysis explored the nature of ordinary, everyday
interactions (Goffman 1983; Sacks 1984). Though from the early years of
work in this tradition and recently, increasingly, the approach has also
been used to research institutional talk, in, for example, hospitals, schools
and universities (Schubert et al. 2009; Heritage 2010; Wicaksono and
Zhurauskaya 2011; O'Keeffe and Walsh 2012), and to study interaction in
research interviews (Mazeland and ten Have 1996; Rapley 2001; Garton
and Copland 2010; Roulston 2010; Talmy 2011).

Many of the institution-focused studies have yielded insights into interactional practices within the research site, and a distinction between so-
called pure conversation analysis and applied conversation analysis has
developed, described by ten Have (2007) as follows:

> In 'pure CA', the focus is on the local practices of turn-taking, sequential
> organisation, etc., in and for themselves, while in 'applied CA' attention
> shifts to the tensions between those local practices and any 'larger struc-
> tures' in which these are embedded, such as institutional rules, institutions,
> accounting, obligations, etc. (ten Have 2007: 199)

Charles Antaki (2011) outlines six kinds of applied conversation
analysis:

- *foundational*, where the approach is used to re-specify the founda-
  tions of established areas of scholarship;

- *social-problem oriented*, where conversation analysis helps to study social issues of communication;
- *communicational*, where the approach offers an alternative analysis of communication problems;
- *diagnostic*, where conversation analysis is used to correlate features of talk with psychological disorders;
- *institutional*, where conversation analysis is used to study interactions in professional communities, for example, hospitals or classrooms;
- *interventional*, where conversation analysis is applied to pre-existing interactional problems with the view to offer recommendations and bring about change.

Conversation analysis offers a unique perspective on the analysis of interview data. One of its advantages, as suggested by Richards (2005), is that it allows analysts to focus their attention on very small features of interaction: the delicate mechanics of the design and management of talk and the effects of those mechanics on the overall interaction. The starting point for much conversation analysis is the turn-taking system. The main principle of this system is that one party speaks at a time, one after the other. Interviews are made up of what seems like a very obvious sequence of turns: questions followed by answers. Unlike many other types of interactions, in which all involved interlocutors are free to initiate new topics or make diverse contributions to the subject, interviews are constrained by the question and answer structure that makes interviews recognisable as such. In interviews, these cultural conventions require that interactional opportunities are pre-allocated in such a way that the interviewers are restricted to questioning and interviewees to answering questions. Sacks (1992, cited in Lobley 2001: 119) calls this a 'chaining rule', meaning that a speaker who asks a question potentially reserves the right to ask another question after the other speaker has finished talking. While this chaining rule gives an overall impression of what we (as members of our discourse community) recognise as an 'interview', closer analysis can show that question and answer sequences are much more complex than we might expect at first hearing or seeing (depending on whether the mode of interaction is speech or sign). In other words, the appropriateness of the questions, and the expectation of a (particular type of) answer, are aspects of (potentially contestable) conventions that must be negotiated in real time by the participants (Clayman and Heritage 2002: 96).

In the case study reported here, we use analytical techniques that are most closely related to the interventional form of applied conversation analysis (Antaki 2011: 8). This part of our data analysis, reported in Chap. 4 of this book, was something that we did in response to our own interest in interaction and in the potential benefits of raising awareness (ours, our students, the leaders of the York's Hidden Stories project) of the features of interaction. And not just the features of an interaction but on the effects these features might have on how the interaction plays out—with consequences for individuals, relationships and the creation/maintenance/resistance of institutional categories/structures: researcher versus participant, teacher versus student, local versus foreign and so on.

In Chap. 5 we explore some of these conventionally accepted binaries and point to a possible way forward for applied linguists who are interested in thinking beyond these.

DISCIPLINARY CONTEXT

In this section, we explore the disciplinary context in which we are working, applied linguistics, and comment on the extent to which various approaches to interviewing could achieve the aims of our discipline.

As the brief list of textbooks that cover their conduct and analysis suggests, above, interviews have been used throughout the social sciences as a way of collecting research data. As far as their theorisation is concerned, their use, both as a method of data collection and a methodology, is a topic of research in a number of branches of the social sciences, including discursive psychology, sociology, anthropology, linguistic anthropology, ethnography, linguistic ethnography and applied linguistics. In this section, we focus on our 'home' discipline, applied linguistics, the disciplinary context for the case study reported in this book.

Applied linguistics has been defined as

> a discipline concerned with the role language and languages play in perceived problems of communication, social identity, education, health, economics, politics and justice, *and* in the development of ways to remediate or resolve these problems'. (Hall et al. 2017: 15)

Hall et al. (2017: 17) present four ingredients that constitute an applied linguistic enquiry: (1) centrality of client needs, (2) pragmatic orientation, (3) social and cognitive embeddedness and, (4) role-shifting and collaboration. In the next part of this section, we explore how three of these four ingredients apply to the community project that is the basis of the research reported in this book.

Centrality of Client Needs

Clients are defined as 'users and beneficiaries of the theoretical knowledge and practical know-how yielded by research in linguistics and applied linguistics' (Hall et al. 2017: 53). In the case of the case study reported in this book, the client is the Centre for Global Education York. The community project set up and run by the Centre was initiated as a follow-up from a study of York's population (Craig et al. 2010). As part of the community project, project workers associated with the Centre conducted a series of interviews with a number of York's Black, Asian and Minority Ethnic residents. Thereafter, the Centre commissioned what they called a thematic analysis of those interviews, providing the need for us to conduct the first part of the study reported in this book.

Applied linguistics is a problem-solving discipline concerned with the identification of solutions for language-related problems, informed by the people who are experiencing the problem (Roberts et al. 1992; Cameron et al. 1992; Brumfit 1995). As far as this study is concerned, the real-world 'problem' was the need, identified by the client, for a thematic analysis of the interviews they had collected. We aimed to provide, therefore, a 'thematic' analysis of interviews with the Black, Asian and Minority Ethnic participants, guided by our client's needs. In addition, we undertook to look closely at the interview techniques used by the project workers. We added this stage to our study with a view to informing the practice of community project interviewing in the future. We say more about the specific challenge of integrating these two very different perspectives on interviews, and the more general challenge of working with clients, in Chap. 5.

Pragmatic Orientation

A second ingredient of an applied linguistic investigation is its pragmatic orientation. In other words, researchers working within applied linguistics should strive to draw on a variety of expertise, in order to solve the language-related problems presented by their client (Hall et al. 2017: 18). Consistent with this pragmatic orientation, this study explores the use of interviews from several of the approaches that we outlined in an earlier section of this chapter. We also look at the interview data using what our client identified as 'thematic analysis', as well as doing an (applied) conversation analysis of the interview techniques and the effects they have on the interaction (including the implications of these effects for the 'findings' of the thematic analysis).

Collaboration

Another ingredient of an applied linguistic project, as suggested by Hall et al. (2017: 18), is collaboration on, for example, research design, data analysis and presentation of findings. The case study reported in this book involved working with the leaders of a community project on all these aspects of the study, in order to provide them with some information in a format that they requested and could use in their project reports, and in the hope of generating critical insights into the interview data, as well as practical recommendations for conducting interviews in the future.

Conclusion

In this chapter, we have presented neo-positivist, romantic, constructionist and transformative reasons for conducting interviews as more or less incompatible. But there are initiatives that are oriented towards bridging the gap between these positions. Hammersley and Atkinson (2019) explore 'reflexivity' in interviewing, an approach which takes into account the role of the interviewers in producing the outcomes of ethnographic interviews. Establishing the 'subject positioning' of the interviewer through the use of a 'bracketing interview' prior to conducting an interview (Roulston 2010: 124) is one possible way in which this might be achieved. Another initiative, also mentioned by van den Berg et al. (2003: 5), is Holstein and Gubrium's (1995) 'active interview', in which both the interviewer and interviewee are acknowledged to play a creative role. There is further rationale for the acknowledgement of the influencing role of the interviewer's talk, and a practical technique (in applied conversation analysis) for the analysis of this role of the interviewer, in Richards (2011).

Going beyond reflexivity and creativity, van den Berg et al. (2003: 5) cite Schuman (1982) on how the interaction between the interviewer and the interviewee is not seen as a methodological problem, but as an opportunity to obtain information about an interviewee's context-dependent behaviour. In other words, the researcher is able to notice the interactional consequences of the interviewer's talk and any other aspects of the context made relevant by the interviewee. In doing so, the researcher has access to information about what the interviewee believes to be the nature of their situation and how they are adapting to it. This is a topic that we return to in Chap. 5 of this book when we offer our recommendations for interviewers interested in the stories that their interviewees tell and in the use of these stories for the potential benefit of the interviewees. We also acknowledge the tendency for some scholars to defend the boundaries of their approach and associated methods, and point to a possible way out of these 'good/bad' uses of methods that goes beyond gap bridging and towards a new understanding of methodological difference.

References

Antaki, C. (2011). Six kinds of applied conversation analysis. In C. Antaki (Ed.), *Applied conversation analysis: Intervention and change in institutional talk.* Houndmills, Basingstoke: Palgrave Macmillan.

Atkinson, P., & Silverman, D. (1997). Kundera's immortality: The interview society and the invention of the self. *Qualitative Inquiry, 3*(3), 304–325.

Attride-Stirling, J. (2001). Thematic networks: An analytic tool for qualitative research. *Qualitative Research, 1*(3), 385–405.

Banglastories. (n.d.). *Interviewing your own family.* LSE/Runnymede Trust. [Online]. Retrieved May 5, 2020, from http://www.banglastories.org/about-the-project/interviewing-your-own-family.html.

Bartlett, J. G., Iwasaki, Y., Gottlieb, B., Hall, D., & Mannell, R. (2007). Framework for aboriginal-guided decolonizing research involving Métis and First Nations persons with diabetes. *Social Science & Medicine, 65*, 2371–2382.

BBC. (2019). *Academy: Journalism/Skills/Interviewing.* [Online]. Retrieved May 5, 2020, from https://www.bbc.co.uk/academy/en.

Boyatzis, R. E. (1998). *Transforming qualitative information: Thematic analysis and code development.* London: Sage.

Braun, V., & Clarke, V. (2006). Using thematic analysis in psychology. *Qualitative Research in Psychology, 3*(2), 77–101.

Braun, V., & Clarke, V. (2019). Reflecting on reflexive thematic analysis. *Qualitative Research in Sport, Exercise and Health, 11*(4), 589–597.

Briggs, C. (2007). Anthropology, interviewing, and communicability in contemporary society. *Current Anthropology, 48*(4), 555–580.

Brinkmann, S. (2018). The interview. In N. K. Denzin & Y. S. Lincoln (Eds.), *The Sage handbook of qualitative research* (pp. 576–599). SAGE: Los Angeles.

Brinkmann, S., & Kvale, S. (2015). *InterViews: Learning the craft of qualitative research interviewing* (3rd ed.). Los Angeles: Sage.

Brumfit, C. J. (1995). Teacher professionalism and research. In G. Cook & B. Seidlhofer (Eds.), *Principle and practice in applied linguistics*. Oxford: Oxford University Press.

Cameron, D., Frazer, E., Harvey, P., Rampton, M. B. H., & Richardson, K. (1992). *Researching language: Issues of power and method*. New York: Routledge.

Cicourel, A. V. (1964). *Method and measurement in sociology*. New York: Free Press.

Clark, H. H., & Schober, M. F. (1992). Asking questions and influencing answers. In J. M. Tanur (Ed.), *Questions about questions* (pp. 15–48). New York: Russell Sage Foundation.

Clayman, S. E., & Heritage, J. (2002). *The news interview: Journalists and public figures on the air*. Cambridge: Cambridge University Press.

Craig, G., Adamson, S., Ali, N., & Demsash, F. (2010). *Mapping rapidly changing minority ethnic populations: A case study of York*. Joseph Rowntree Foundation. [Online]. Retrieved March 20, 2019, from www.jrf.org.uk/publications/changing-minority-ethnic-populations.

De Fina, A., & Georgakopoulou, A. (2008). Analysing narratives as practices. *Qualitative Research, 8*(3), 379–387.

De Fina, A., & Perrino, S. (2011). Introduction: Interviews vs. 'natural' contexts: A false dilemma. *Language in Society, 40*(1), 1–11.

Fairclough, N., & Wodak, R. (1997). Critical discourse analysis. In T. Van Dijk (Ed.), *Discourse studies: A multidisciplinary introduction*. London: Sage.

Garfinkel, H. (1967). *Studies in ethnomethodology*. Englewood Cliffs, NJ: Prentice Hall.

Garton, S., & Copland, F. (2010). 'I like this interview; I get cakes and cats!': The effect of prior relationships on interview talk. *Qualitative Research, 10*(5), 533–551.

Gibbs, G. R. (2007). Thematic coding and categorizing. In *Analyzing qualitative data*. London: Sage.

Goffman, E. (1983). The interaction order. *American Sociological Review, 48*, 1–17.

Gubrium, J., Holstein, J. A., Marvasti, A. B., & McKinney, A. D. (Eds.). (2012). *The Sage handbook of interviewing: The complexity of the craft*. Thousand Oaks: Sage.

Hall, C. J., Smith, P. H., & Wicaksono, R. (2017). *Mapping applied linguistics: An introduction for students and practitioners*. Abingdon: Routledge.

Hammersley, M. & Atkinson, P. (2019). *Ethnography: Principles in practice*. Abingdon, Routledge.

ten Have, P. (2007). *Doing conversation analysis: A practical guide*. London: Sage.

Heritage, J. (2010). Questioning in medicine. In A. Freed & S. Ehrlich (Eds.), *Why do you ask?: The function of questions in institutional discourse*. New York: Oxford University Press.

Hollway, W. (2005). Commentary. *Qualitative Research in Psychology, 2*, 312–314.

Holstein, J. A., & Gubrium, J. F. (1995). Qualitative research methods, Vol. 37. *The active interview*. Thousand Oaks: Sage.

Holstein, J. A., & Gubrium, J. F. (2000). *The self we live by: Narrative identity in a postmodern world*. Oxford: Oxford University Press.

Holstein, J. A., & Gubrium, J. F. (2004). The active interview. In D. Silverman (Ed.), *Qualitative research: Theory, method and practice* (2nd ed.). London: Sage.

Kvale, S. (2007). *Doing interviews*. London: Sage.

Labov, W., & Waletzky, J. (1967). Narrative analysis: Oral versions of Personal Experience. In J. Helm (Ed.), *Essays on the verbal and visual arts* (pp. 12–44). Seattle: University of Washington.

Lobley, L. (2001). Whose personality is it anyway? The production of 'Personality' in a diagnostic interview. In A. McHoul & M. Rapley (Eds.), *How to analyse talk in institutional settings*. London: Continuum.

Mann, S. (2011). A critical review of qualitative interviews in applied linguistics. *Applied Linguistics, 32*(1), 6–24.

Mann, S. (2016). *The research interview: Reflective practice and reflexivity in research processes*. Basingstoke: Palgrave Macmillan.

Marn, T., & Wolgemuth, J. R. (2017). Purposeful entanglements: A new materialist analysis of transformative interviews. *Qualitative Inquiry, 23*(5), 365–374.

Mazeland, H., & ten Have, P. (1996). Essential tensions in (semi-) open research interviews. In I. Maso & D. Wester (Eds.), *The deliberate dialogue: Qualitative perspectives on the interview*. Brussels: VUB University Press.

O'Keeffe, A., & Walsh, S. (2012). Applying corpus linguistics and conversation analysis in the investigation of small group teaching in Higher Education. *Corpus Linguistics and Linguistic Theory, 8*(1), 159–181.

Oral History Project: Giving Voice to the American Latino Experience. (2015). *'Learn to Interview', 'How to Video' and 'How to Kit'*. University of Texas Libraries: University of Texas, Austin, USA. [Online]. Retrieved September 19, 2019, from http://www.lib.utexas.edu/voces/training-index.html.

Rapley, T. J. (2001). The art(fulness) of open-ended interviewing: Some considerations on analysing interviews. *Qualitative Research, 1*(3), 303–323.

Richards, K. (2005). Introduction. In K. Richards & P. Seedhouse (Eds.), *Applying conversation analysis*. Basingstoke: Palgrave Macmillan.

Richards, K. (2011). Using micro-analysis in interviewer training: 'Continuers' and interviewer positioning. *Applied Linguistics, 32*(1), 95–112.

Roberts, C., Davies, E., & Jupp, T. (1992). *Language and discrimination: A study of communication in multi-ethnic workplaces*. Harlow, UK: Longman.

Rodger R. & Herbert J. (Eds.). (2007). *Testimonies of the city: Identity, community and change in a contemporary urban world*. Aldershot: Ashgate Publishing.

Roulston, K. (2010). *Reflective interviewing: A guide to theory and practice*. London: Sage.

Roulston, K. (2011). Interview 'problems' as topics for analysis. *Applied Linguistics, 32*(1), 77–94.

Rubin, H. J., & Rubin, I. S. (2012). *Qualitative interviewing: The art of hearing data* (3rd ed.). Los Angeles: Sage.

Sacks, H. (1984). Notes on methodology. In J. M. Atkinson & J. Heritage (Eds.), *Structures of social action* (pp. 21–27). Cambridge: Cambridge University Press.

Schostak, J. (2006). *Interviewing and representation in qualitative research.* Maidenhead, UK: Open University Press.

Schuman, H. (1982). Artifacts are in the mind of the beholder. *American Sociologist, 17*(1), 21–8.

Schubert, S. J., Hansen, S., Dyer, K. R., & Rapley, M. (2009). "'ADHD patient" or "illicit drug user"? Managing medico-moral membership categories in drug dependence services. *Discourse and Society, 20*(4), 499–516.

Seidman, I. (2012). *Interviewing as qualitative research: A guide for researchers in education and the social sciences* (4th ed.). New York: Teachers College.

Silverman, D. (2004). Foreword. In B. Czarniawska (Ed.), *Narratives in social science research.* London: Sage.

Silverman, D. (Ed.). (2010). *Qualitative research: Theory, method and practice.* London: Sage.

Silverman, D. (2013). *Doing qualitative research: A practical handbook* (4th ed.). London: Sage.

Silverman, D. (2015). *Interpreting qualitative data: Methods for analysing talk, text and interaction* (5th ed.). Thousand Oaks: Sage.

Talmy, S. (2010). Qualitative interviews in applied linguistics: From research instrument to social practice. *Annual Review of Applied Linguistics, 30*, 128–148.

Talmy, S. (2011). The interview as collaborative achievement: Interaction, identity and ideology in a speech event. *Applied Linguistics, 32*(1), 25–42.

Talmy, S., & Richards, K. (2010). Theorizing qualitative research interviews in applied linguistics. *Applied Linguistics, 32*(1), 1–5.

The East Midlands Oral History Archive. (n.d.). *How do I conduct an oral history interview?* Centre for Urban History, University of Leicester: Leicester. [Online]. Retrieved January 28, 2020, from https://www.le.ac.uk/emoha/training/no2.pdf.

Tuckett, A. G. (2005). Applying thematic analysis theory to practice: A researcher's experience. *Contemporary Nurse, 19*(1–2), 75–87.

Usher, R. (1996). A critique of the neglected epistemological assumptions of educational research. In D. Scott & R. Usher (Eds.), *Understanding educational research.* London; New York: Routledge.

Van den Berg, H., Wetherell, M., & Houtkoop-Steenstra, H. (Eds.). (2003). *Analyzing race talk: Multidisciplinary approaches to the interview.* Cambridge: Cambridge University Press.

Veterans History Project. (2005). *Sample interview questions for veterans.* American Folklife Center: Library of Congress, USA. [Online]. Retrieved September 10, 2019, from http://www.loc.gov/vets/questions.html.

Wicaksono, R., & Zhurauskaya, D. (2011). *Introducing English as a Lingua Franca: An online tutorial.* [Online]. Retrieved June 28, 2016, from www.englishlinguafranca.com.

CHAPTER 2

Community Projects and Hidden Stories

Abstract This chapter presents a number of community-based projects that have used interviews to discover the stories of people in a particular location or who are considered part of a group. The chapter introduces the case study on which the book is based: York's Hidden Stories (YHS). YHS was a community research project run by the Centre for Global Education York, and involved people who were born outside the UK and had moved to York. In reporting on this project, the aim of the study is to provide a 'real-world' illustration of some different approaches to interviews as research data, as well as how these approaches might meet the requirements of applied linguist(ic)s.

Keywords Partnership • Community-Based projects • Migration • Hidden stories

The case study we outline in this chapter explores a partnership between applied linguists, who research and teach at a university, and a community organisation (hereafter referred to as 'the client'): the Centre for Global Education York. Prior to the contact with the university, the client had conducted semi-structured interviews with fifteen Black, Asian and Minority Ethnic residents of York, as part of the York's Hidden Stories project, and was seeking an analysis of these interviews. The outcome of our applied linguistics study was a synopsis of the interview analysis and a

R. Wicaksono, D. Zhurauskaya, *York's Hidden Stories*,
https://doi.org/10.1057/978-1-137-55839-8_2

series of recommendations for data collection and analysis, aimed at interviewers working on similar community projects.

The research reported here will henceforth be referred to as an applied linguistic 'study'. The York's Hidden Stories project that provided the data for the study will be referred as a community 'project'.

The remainder of this chapter covers information about the client and the context that frames this study, as well as an account of other, similar, studies. Also included in the chapter are the research questions that the study aimed to answer.

Community Projects, Interviews and Hidden Stories (of Migration)

Collecting peoples' stories is a common aim of both academic research and community projects. Often, such stories are collected with a view to capturing and sharing the heritage of people and places, as part of oral history projects. Using interviews as a way to elicit the 'real' lives of people, who are perhaps all living in one 'place' (in the case of the study reported here, a city), requires belief in interview data as true confession. This 'romantic' approach to interviews (as we argued in Chap. 1) assumes that an interviewee's answers provide insight into their life-world that is authentic and which might not be available to the public without the interaction with the interviewer. In all of the examples below, except perhaps the *Stanford Storytelling Project*, the aim of the interviews was to collect these previously 'hidden' true confessions. The *Stanford Storytelling Project* had more of a constructionist/transformative aim, acknowledging that interviews are context-bound co-constructions that may have the power to change the lives of the interviewees (ideally for the better). In this section we compare the uses of (and implied beliefs about) interviews in projects designed to reveal, or create, stories.

Examples of hybrid academic/community projects using interviews to elicit hidden stories in the UK include the University of Sheffield's *Storying Sheffield* (n.d.), which aims to document local heritage through a wide range of means, with a view to creating a true representation of life in Sheffield. The *Storying Sheffield* project team collect stories from people with disabilities, senior citizens, school students and new migrants to the city, stories that, without the intervention of the project, might be invisible to the people who are not members of these groups. Another storytelling initiative based in the University of Sheffield is the Youzi Project (n.d.), which explores the Chinese student community in the city. The project is a collaboration between a photographer, an academic and students at the University, where students' stories published on the project website are also accompanied by images and video recordings. *Bangla Stories* (n.d.), another example from the UK, is a collaboration between the London School of Economics, the University of Cambridge and the Runnymede Trust (an independent race equality think tank). As part of a three-year study, 180 life history interviews with first-generation migrants living in India, Bangladesh and the UK were collected. The project website, aimed at school teachers and their pupils, describes how the resulting stories 'paint a very intimate portrait of what it means to migrate, to start a new life and create a new home'. It is these 'intimate' details in the stories of individual migrants that aim to challenge over-generalised, potentially dehumanising, assumptions about migration, raising awareness of hitherto 'hidden' aspects of the lives of the interviewees and changing public attitudes.

In addition to university-based projects such as these, stories are also collected by media organisations and community projects. KALW, a public radio station based in San Francisco, for example, runs a storytelling project called *Hear Here* (KALW 2014). Also in the USA, *StoryCorps* (n.d.) has recorded the stories of around a quarter of a million people, published the recordings online and archived them at the Library of Congress. In the UK, BBC Radio Four hosts a similar storytelling show, *The Listening Project* (n.d.), in which friends or members of a family are invited to record an unrehearsed conversation about a true experience, sections of which are broadcast with only very brief introductions from the programme host. Also in the UK, the National Lottery sponsors organisations through the Heritage Lottery Fund to run community-based projects that aim to explore, share and celebrate the diverse heritage of the UK through oral storytelling.

Storytelling projects are not always (exclusively) oral. One of the most well-known examples of a community storytelling project is *Humans of New York* (n.d.), which began in 2010 as a series of photographs. The project started with the goal of collecting 10,000 photographs of residents of New York for a catalogue of the city's inhabitants. The project founder, who is also the project photographer, Brandon Stanton, soon started to interview his subjects, in addition to taking their photograph, and began to publish snippets of peoples' stories alongside the photographs. *Humans of New York* now has over twenty-five million followers on social media and is a global multi-media platform for sharing the stories of some of the people that can be seen on the streets of New York as well as stories the project founder collected on their travel and a series of stories focusing on specific populations, for example, paediatric cancer patients, inmates and refugee stories. The popularity of *Humans of New York* online has prompted the creation of similar-looking 'humans of' projects in other cities, regions and workplaces around the world. For example, the *Humans of Leeds* (2020), *Humans of London* (Teesdale 2016), *Humans of University* (2020), *Humans of Bombay* (2020), *Humans of Scotland* (The Alliance 2019) and *Humans of Fashion*. These, and other, 'Humans of' projects, despite their similar-looking format of 'photo + story', have quite a wide range of aims, including to celebrate the diversity of a city's life, create a database for a dating website, address social issues or give residents of a place an opportunity to share their opinions on various topics.

In contrast with the examples above, the *Stanford Storytelling Project* (n.d.), run by Stanford University in the USA, is advertised as a series of workshops to help students and staff 'learn the craft of storytelling', treating stories as 'creations' rather than simply as 'collectables'. The project website emphasises this aspect, 'Our mission is to promote the transformative nature of traditional and modern oral storytelling, from Lakota tales to Radiolab, and empower students to create and perform their own stories'.

As we said in Chap. 1, interviews to elicit stories are widely used in both academic and everyday contexts. The popularity of interviews seems mainly to be based on the naturalistic assumption that interviewing is either a neutral or a confessional activity and that the previously hidden stories are revealed (and then collected) by the interview(er). As our final example shows, there may also be projects that use interviews to achieve very different aims, namely, the exploration of the creative and transformative power of stories, based on the contrasting assumption that stories are not neutral accounts of a past, but new versions of people and events that create new pasts, and the potential for different futures.

In the next section of this chapter, we describe the background to the storytelling project that we worked on, including its aims and assumptions about its methods.

A Case Study of a Community Project

The community project that formed the basis of our study was initiated as a response to research commissioned by the Joseph Rowntree Foundation's York Grants Committee in 2010. The research aimed to give a more accurate picture of York's Black, Asian and Minority Ethnic population and to make related recommendations to local authorities. The results of the research revealed that York's population was much more diverse than had previously been suggested, identifying seventy-eight different minority first languages spoken in the city and estimating the Minority Ethnic population at approximately eleven per cent of York's total population. This figure was higher than that suggested by the 2001 census, in which only 2.1 per cent of respondents identified themselves as not White or White other and 4.9 per cent as not White British, a much lower percentage than the UK average. These results were confirmed by statistics published from the 2011 census, which confirmed that 90.2 per cent of York's population identified themselves as White British. In the report on their research, Craig et al. emphasised the need for York to strengthen its commitment to racial equality and diversity, with a view to making a positive impact on the lives of Minority Ethnic groups in the city.

The Centre for Global Education York, the initiators of the community project that provides the case study explored in this book, is a charity that works with the local community to offer support and training aimed at developing understanding of global issues. More specifically, it 'aims to provide support, challenge, training and learning opportunities that allow interactive involvement with a variety of global educational projects and events' (Centre for Global Education York 2014). The Centre has been running for more than thirty years, and for the past twenty years has been based at York St John University. As a 'not-for-profit organisation', it is overseen by a group of voluntary directors, and its work is delivered by self-employed associates who manage grant-funded projects (Centre for Global Education York 2014). The work of the Centre is mainly carried out in local schools, colleges and universities. In 2012–14, the Centre engaged with a wider audience through the community-based York's Hidden Stories project, funded by the Joseph Rowntree Foundation, Comic Relief, Community York, and York St John University.

The York's Hidden Stories project was a response to the research, cited above, that emphasised the need for York to strengthen its commitment to racial equality and diversity (Craig et al. 2010). The aim of the project was to capture and share the stories of York's Black, Asian and Minority Ethnic residents, and involved fifteen participants who were interviewed about their experiences of moving to, and living in, York. On completion of the project, the project leaders' evaluation suggested that their project had 'recorded, shared and celebrated the cultural heritage of York's unseen and often unknown multicultural community that could result in disadvantage', noting that, 'these individuals (the Black, Asian and Minority Ethnic participants) were trained to impart their unique cultural memories and experiences which are now part of York's Community'.

The data that was used in our study consists of audio recordings of semi-structured interviews that were collected by the Centre for Global Education York as part of the York's Hidden Stories project. In total, there are fifteen interviews in which one interviewee and two project leaders participate. Each interview lasts approximately one hour. Each participant was asked the same set of questions; see Chap. 3—Methodology—covering general information about the participant, their values, their life in their country of origin and the changes they may have experienced since coming to York. The interviews aimed to provide an insight into peoples' memories of their 'home' countries, and their experience of moving to and living in York.

MIGRATION AND HIDDEN STORIES

The choice of the word 'hidden' for the title of the project designed and run by the Centre was a response to the recommendations of the research conducted by Craig et al. (2010). As mentioned earlier in this chapter, this research found, and the 2011 census later confirmed, that York was more diverse than had previously been supposed. The report recommended that more should be done to highlight the actual ethnic diversity of York, concluding that,

> Most obviously, York is a substantially more diverse city in terms of the ethnic origins of its population (even allowing for the transitory nature of some, generally small, populations). This should be acknowledged and celebrated publicly in terms of politics and policy and by the media. (Craig et al. 2010:43)

The Craig report uses the word 'hidden' to describe the population of workers in the city whose labour is not seen because such work often takes place in the evenings or at night (in occupations such as cleaners, caretakers or domestic/residential carers) or in 'backroom' jobs in hotels, bars and restaurants. Amongst other effects of this 'hiddenness', according to the Craig report, is that actual ethnic diversity is also hidden, potentially having a further homogenising effect on the city:

> One clear reason why many [Black, Asian and Minority Ethnic workers] in, for example, the restaurant trade, do not live in the city is because it is still seen, culturally and in terms of services and policies, as a 'White city'. (Craig et al. 2010: 43)

The community project that generated the data we analysed for our study was a direct response to the Craig report and, as such, it aimed to 'unhide' the stories of the participants by making their memories and experiences part of the (previously unseen) history of the city. Out of respect for the aims of the community project that made our study possible, we chose to re-use the word 'hidden' in the title of this book. As our review of the various approaches to research interviews in Chap. 1 shows, there is a way of thinking about the purpose of interviews that assumes they can provide access to the 'real' experiences of interviewees—and that interviews can uncover truths that were previously hidden, until they were elicited by a skilful interviewer. In the next chapter, we say more about our analytic methods and how we conducted a neo-positivist/romantic thematic analysis alongside a more constructionist analysis of the talk itself. Constructionist ideas about interviews, as we say in Chap. 1, treat the interviewer and interviewee as in interaction with each other and their context. From a constructionist perspective, we were also able to see the recordings as examples of how life stories get constructed (and distributed) and to speculate on the possible consequences for the storytellers. In this sense, the stories were not so much 'unhidden' as 're-made', with a specific audience in mind and in interaction with that audience. From this perspective, the interview became a site of struggle for the 'right story', a good story, a true story, an acceptable story, all according to the participants in the event.

Whether the accounts of the participants in the community project are conceptualised as 'unhidden' or 're-made' does not affect the result of the interviews, which was to circulate York's migration stories and highlight the ethnic diversity of the city, as recommended by the Craig report. On the other hand, studies by Blommaert (2001) and Smith-Khan (2017) have made the important point that interviews with migrants who are seeking asylum can have life-changing consequences for the interviewees. In such cases, the interviewees, and the scholars that study the recordings of interaction in these high stakes' contexts, cannot afford to be as sanguine about the structural challenges, power dynamics and resulting (lack of) opportunities for the exercise of agency of the interview as perhaps we were.

RESEARCH QUESTIONS

The aim of the study reported in this book was to explore the partnership between applied linguists and a client, in this case, a local community organisation, the Centre for Global Education York. The client provided the data for the study, which comprised fifteen (approximately one-hour-long) interviews, conducted by community organisation workers, who were themselves members of York's Black, Asian and Minority Ethnic community.

The Centre for Global Education requested transcriptions and interpretation of their interview recordings on topics specified by them, which they planned to use to report back to the project funders and to justify future funding. This request provided a rationale for the first research question asked by the study. In addition, and separately from the requests made by the client, the researchers were interested in the use of interviews as a data collection tool and in the potential for the study to result in a set of recommendations for community project workers conducting interviews for projects of a similar nature. This interest provided a rationale for the second research question asked by the study.

Based on these requests/interests, the following two research questions were asked:

1. What themes occur in the interviews with York's Black, Asian and Minority Ethnic residents, on the topics identified by the client?
2. How do the interviewers' contributions shape the interaction with the interviewees?

Research question one is based on the aim of the community project to 'unhide' the stories of the Black, Asian and Minority Ethnic community in York. Research question two is based on the complementary idea of 're-making' stories.

The Craig report (2010) comments that the changes to the ethnic diversity of the city of York, and the hidden nature of these changes, are likely to mirror those taking place in other small cities or large towns in the UK, such as Chester, Exeter, Gloucester, Lancaster, Lincoln or Norwich. In the same way that the Craig report's implications for the city of York are likely to be relevant for these other places, it is hoped that the findings of this study might be usable in other, similar, contexts in the UK and around the world in towns and cities with (somewhat) mobile populations.

In the next chapter of this book, we present the methodological choices we made. We also describe our data in more detail, and outline how we used both thematic analysis and conversation analysis. The transcription conventions used, and some of the ethical questions raised by our research, will also be considered.

References

Banglastories. (n.d.). *Interviewing your own family*. LSE/Runnymede Trust. [Online]. Retrieved May 5, 2020, from http://www.banglastories.org/about-the-project/interviewing-your-own-family.html.

BBC Radio 4. (n.d.). *The Listening Project*. [Online]. Retrieved July 21, 2019, from http://www.bbc.co.uk/programmes/b01cqx3b.

Blommaert, J. (2001). Investigating narrative inequality: African asylum seekers' stories in Belgium. *Discourse & Society, 12*(4), 413–449.

Centre for Global Education York. (2014). [Online]. Retrieved July 2, 2019, from https://www.theCentreforGlobalEducationYorkork.org.

Craig, G., Adamson, S., Ali, N., & Demsash, F. (2010). *Mapping rapidly changing minority ethnic populations: A case study of York*. Joseph Rowntree Foundation. [Online]. Retrieved March 20, 2019, from www.jrf.org.uk/publications/changing-minority-ethnic-populations.

Humans of Bombay. (2020). [Instagram]. Retrieved May 5, 2020, from https://www.instagram.com/officialhumansofbombay/?hl=en.

Humans of Leeds. (2020). [Instagram]. Retrieved May 5, 2020, from https://www.instagram.com/humansofleeds/?hl=en.

Humans of New York. (n.d.). [Online]. Retrieved May 5, 2020, from www.humansofnewyork.com.

Humans of University. (2020). [Instagram]. Retrieved May 5, from https://www.instagram.com/humansofuniversity/?hl=en.

KALW. (2014). *Hear Here*. [Online]. Retrieved May 5, 2020, from www.kalw.org/topic/hear-here.

Smith-Khan, L. (2017). Negotiating narratives, accessing asylum: Evaluating language policy as multi-level practice, beliefs and management. *Multilingua, 36*, 31–57.

StoryCorps. (n.d.). [Online]. Retrieved July 17, 2019, from https://storycorps.org.

Storying Sheffield Telling Untold Stories. (n.d.). [Online]. Retrieved February 10, 2019, from www.storyingsheffield.com.

Teesdale, C. (2016). *Humans of London.* London: LOM Art.

The ALLIANCE. (2019). *Humans of Scotland.* [Online]. Retrieved May 5, 2020, from https://www.alliance-scotland.org.uk/wp-content/uploads/2019/09/HOS-Ebook.pdf.

The Stanford Storytelling Project. (n.d.). [Online]. Retrieved May 5, 2020, from https://storytelling.stanford.edu.

Youzi Project. (n.d.). [Online]. Retrieved February 10, 2019, from www.youziproject.com.

CHAPTER 3

Methodology

Abstract This chapter provides details about the study's research methodology. It begins with a detailed description of the participants in the interviews and of the data that was generated. The chapter discusses the use of two methods used in the analysis of the interview data: thematic analysis and conversation analysis. Transcription conventions and the ethical challenges of the case study are also explored in this chapter.

Keywords Method • Research questions • Data • Participants • Transcription

INTRODUCTION

This chapter provides details about the research methods of the case study reported here. The chapter begins with a description of the data which was used for the analysis presented in Chap. 4. There were two research questions asked in the case study, each of which required two different approaches to data analysis:

1. What themes occur in the interviews with York's Black, Asian and Minority Ethnic residents on the topics identified by the client?
2. How do the interviewers' contributions shape the interaction with the interviewees?

© The Author(s) 2020
R. Wicaksono, D. Zhurauskaya, *York's Hidden Stories*,
https://doi.org/10.1057/978-1-137-55839-8_3

Research question one was approached with what the project leaders, our clients, called a 'thematic analysis', whereas research question two required a conversation analytic approach. Those two data analysis approaches are presented in the middle section of this chapter, followed by a description of the two transcription conventions that were used to transcribe the data. The remaining section of the chapter discusses some of the ethical issues which were presented by our study.

THE DATA

The case study used data collected by the Centre for Global Education as part of the York's Hidden Stories project and consisted of fifteen semi-structured interviews, conducted by two project leaders who were both present at each interview, with the fifteen project participants. All the participants had been living in York for between two and fifty years and had originally come to York from Africa, Asia, Latin America, the Caribbean or Europe.

The project participants took part in the York's Hidden Stories project through a series of workshops over the course of six months. During that time the participants 'were trained to impart their unique cultural memories and experiences which are now part of York's Community' (Centre for Global Education York 2014). Towards the end of the community project, the participants were interviewed by the project leaders. Each participant was asked the following set of twenty-five questions (and some were asked additional questions):

1. Where are you from?
2. Tell us about your name, what does it mean?
3. Where do you get your values from?
4. What do you treasure the most in life?
5. Has coming to York changed your values and what you treasure?
6. What do you treasure the most about your home country?
7. What do you treasure about York?
8. Is there anything you feel you need in life?
9. If I could grant you a wish, what would it be for you and for the world?
10. What skills, talents and gifts do you think you have?

11. Do you think those skills have been helpful during your life in York? If you haven't come to live in York, do you think you would be a different person?
12. What differences do you see in citizens from your country and here in the UK?
13. Who do you think you are?
14. What were your first impressions of York?
15. Was it easy to move to York?
16. When you arrived in York, were there any people who helped you?
17. If you could bring something from home to York, what would it be?
18. If you could take something back home from York, what would it be?
19. Do you think there is anything distinctive about people in York/Yorkshire?
20. Are there any barriers you had to overcome in life?
21. What helped you to overcome barriers?
22. Has living in York created any barriers for you?
23. Has living in York helped you to overcome certain barriers?
24. Do you think in your home country that there are barriers that people have to overcome that are different or the same as for people in the UK?
25. In five years' time, where do you think you will be in life?

Most of the project participants, and both interviewers, were multilingual. All the interviews were conducted in English and audio recorded. The length of the recordings is outlined in Table 3.1.

It is important to note that the interviewees and interviewers were already familiar with each other prior to the interviewing, given that the interviewers had had a chance to build relationships with their interviewees over the course of six months of workshops and events. Garton and Copland (2010) refer to these types of interviews, where there is a prior relationship between interviewers and interviewees, as 'acquaintance interviews'. They stress that a prior relationship, or lack of one, can have a profound effect on the data that gets generated in interview talk and suggest that participants of acquaintance interviews should be made aware of the impact a prior relationship may have on the interaction. Mann (2016) argues that familiarity can be both an advantage and a disadvantage. Where the interviewer enters into the interaction in the hope of achieving a deeper understanding of their interviewee's perspective (what we describe

Table 3.1   Length of recordings

	Pseudonym	Continent of origin	Interview length
1	Diara	Europe	41 minutes
2	Chardon	Central America	1 hour 2 minutes
3	Bao	Asia	48 minutes
4	Chima	Africa	50 minutes
5	Yun	Asia	50 minutes
6	Chris	Africa	1 hour 7 minutes
7	Zenith	Africa	1 hour 6 minutes
8	Alex	South America	1 hour 34 minutes
9	Jamal	Africa	58 minutes
10	Andri	Asia	50 minutes
11	Michi	Asia	43 minutes
12	Sage	Europe	46 minutes
13	Sasha	Europe	51 minutes
14	Jessi	Europe	1 hour 7 minutes
15	Hanzila	Africa	11 minutes

in Chap. 1 as a 'romantic' assumption), it can help them to feel better able to understand what the interviewee 'really means'. Where the interviewer enters into the interaction with a neo-positivist perspective, familiarity may feel like a disadvantage, in the fear that they will be encouraged to engage with their interviewee's responses through the lens of their own prior experiences. For researchers who enter into an acquaintance interview with a constructionist perspective, familiarity is neither an advantage or a disadvantage, but an inevitable feature of all interaction that is to be noted (and perhaps studied, as part of the analysis of the interview data).

We assume, but can't be sure, that the leaders of the community project that resulted in the fifteen interviews built relationships with the participants through workshop and events in the six months prior in order to deliberately create 'acquaintance' interviews, with a view to achieving a deeper 'understanding' of the stories that were generated. It may be the case, however, that the project leaders built these relationships simply in order to create longer answers, generating more data for analysis, or that they saw the six months of workshops and events held prior to the interviews as a separate stage of the project, with no consequences for the interviews. It is also possible that the project leaders were aware of the transformative power of interviews, aiming to use their interview data and any discussion of their findings to benefit the project participants, by raising awareness of aspects of their lives or challenging interpretations of their experience in order to change the attitudes of their fellow residents of the city of York.

Given that we are now unable to ask our clients about their rationale for the design of their project, we would advise other applied linguists (including ourselves in future) to discuss the design of a project before it begins, so that project leaders, participants and researchers are, as far as possible, aware of the assumptions behind, and the consequences of, their decisions from the very start.

THEMATIC ANALYSIS

We used what the project leaders called 'thematic analysis' to answer research question one of our study, in order to summarise answers on the topics identified by our client.

Thematic analysis is a common way of analysing qualitative data in order to report what seems to the analyst to be the key issues (or 'phenomena') that are present in the data (Gibbs 2007). More specifically, it has been described as a method of 'identifying, analysing and reporting patterns (themes) within data' (Braun and Clarke 2006: 79). In a later version of their 2006 paper, Braun and Clarke (2019) describe a number of different approaches to thematic analysis, which they are keen to delineate, and distinguish 'fully realised themes' from 'confusing summaries of data domains or topics' (2019: 589).

A 'fully realised' approach to thematic analysis is designed to be inductive, or 'bottom-up'. The first stage is usually to code the interview transcript for important words, phrases or ideas. Boyatzis (1998: 63) defines these words, phrases or ideas as 'the most basic segment, or element, of raw data or information that can be assessed in a meaningful way regarding the phenomenon'. These elements are then grouped into larger categories, and the relationships between the elements within the categories, and the categories themselves, are explored. In the presentation of the findings of a thematic analysis, extracts from the data may be used to exemplify the categories of which they form a part. Thematic analysis is usually conducted in the following stages (see Robson 2011):

- Familiarisation with the data: at this stage, the researcher reads and/ or listens to the data a number of times, making notes of initial ideas.

- Generation of initial codes: during this stage, extracts from the data are coded across the dataset, with similar extracts being assigned the same code.
- Identification of themes: this stage involves organising codes into potential themes.
- Construction of thematic networks: at this stage, a thematic map of the data is developed.
- Integration and interpretation: during this stage, the patterning of (or relationship between) the themes is explored, which are then summarised and interpreted with reference to the context of the data and/or other, similar, research findings.

In contrast to this 'bottom-up' approach, in the case study described in this book, the client had already identified three themes prior to our analysis. The themes that were of interest to the client were reasons for immigration to York, participants' values in life and what the participants said about any barriers in their lives. Given that the themes were pre-determined by the client and the analysis was linked to the client's needs, a deductive, or 'top-down', approach to the thematic analysis was conducted. This approach runs the risk of providing 'confusing summaries of data domains or topics' (Braun and Clarke 2019: 589), but it did provide findings in a format that met the needs of our client. Furthermore, when combined with the findings of research question two, we hope that our summaries on the topics identified by the project leaders are shown (including to the project leaders) to be what they 'are': different stories about stories.

Conversation Analysis

Research question two asked: how do the interviewers' contributions shape the interaction with the interviewees? The approach we took to this question is conversation analytic, drawing on the main principles of conversation analysis: turn-taking, turn design and sequential organisation of talk (Sacks et al. 1974). As described in Chap. 1, the main methodological resource of conversation analysis lies in interpreting the understanding of a previous talk in the next turn (Sacks et al. 1974).

The rationale for applying a conversation analysis-informed approach was to enable us to take a very close look at the details of the interview data, in order to study the ways in which specific interactional features had an effect on the progress of the interviews. As described by ten Have

(1990), conversation analysis provides a structured way of studying the details of interactional extracts from a dataset enabling researchers to identify various insights in the data. Research question two required us to look at how the interviews started, and how they moved along, as well as how they got to their end. Conversation analysis's focus on sequences helped us to see how questions led to answers, which in turn led to further questions, allowing us to pay attention to the 'journey' of the stories the participants told.

Based on ten Have's (1990) model, the following six stages were followed in analysing the data for our study.

Stage One

The first step consists of making audio or video recordings of conversations. In the case of our study, this stage was already completed by the project leaders prior to this study, and the recorded interviews were shared with the researchers.

Stage Two

The second step is to produce a transcript of the recordings. There were two different transcriptions made for our study. Firstly, a verbatim transcription of all interviews was produced and shared with the community project leaders. Secondly, selected episodes from verbatim transcriptions were transcribed using conversation analysis transcription conventions. The selection of the episodes for transcription is discussed below.

Stage Three

Stage three involves building a collection of extracts for analysis. There are a number of considerations to be made at this stage. For instance, ten Have (1990) suggests that a good starting point for researchers might be to focus their attention on conversation openings or closings or to select sequential structures with an interesting conversational phenomenon, for example, overlaps, laughter or long pauses. Gail Jefferson referred to such selections as 'virtuoso moments'; these are 'episodes that strike the observer as being carried out in a particularly felicitous manner' (ten Have 2007: 38).

In the case of our study, all the interviews were listened to in order to identify sections of the interviews in which 'values' and 'barriers' were mentioned. In these sections, turn-taking sequences were examined, and interesting conversational phenomena were noted, leading to the selection of five extracts, which are presented for detailed analysis in Chap. 4. The data from the 'reasons for immigration' section was not used because, in the majority of cases, the recordings of the interviews started with participants introducing themselves and explaining their reasons for immigrating. Therefore, there was no interaction between interviewees and interviewers to analyse.

Stage Four

Stage four is concerned with the initial analysis of the selected extracts, with a particular focus on the construction of turns, pauses, overlaps, repair and any other 'disturbances' in the fluent working of the turn-taking system. ten Have (1990: 9) describes this stage as an interpretation of the data which is 'specifically directed at a typification of what the utterances that make up the sequence can be held to be "doing" and how these "doings" interconnect'.

Stage Five

At this stage, further analysis is developed, combining the initial analysis from stage four with the researcher's relevant knowledge about the research participants, in order to develop a more detailed understanding of the selected extracts.

Stage Six

Stage six of our study involved extending the analysis made in steps four and five by comparing our data with similar or dissimilar examples found in other conversation analysis studies. ten Have (1990) highlights the importance of this stage for conversation analysis researchers, as it allows for the building of a collection of similar extracts to support a systematic comparison.

A detailed conversation analysis of five selected extracts from our data is available in Chap. 4 of this book.

TRANSCRIBING SPOKEN DATA

Researchers often talk about making choices about interviewing styles but rarely about the types and levels of transcriptions used when they write out their data. Wetherell (2003: 29) reminds us to pay attention to these choices, saying that 'transcription constructs what the data is'. Although the primary data for this study were audio recordings, transcription was essential in order to be able to report the data to our clients and to help us begin to think about research question two. As Heath and Luff say (1993: 309, cited in ten Have 2007: 96):

> The process of transcription…provides the researcher with a way of noticing, even discovering, particular events, and helps focus analytic attention on their socio-interactional organisation.

The choices that we made about the types and levels of transcription of our data included the level of detail of the transcription (e.g. whether or not to note non-verbal communication), what style of orthography to use ('I won't' versus 'I will not') and the use of punctuation (see Mann 2016). In the end, we used two types of transcription: verbatim transcription, as requested by the client, and some of the transcription conventions associated with conversation analysis, as developed by Gail Jefferson (Jefferson 2004).

Our verbatim transcription is content-focused and uses a limited number of transcription symbols, mainly to capture pauses, overlaps and additional information such as laughter. The verbatim transcription was requested by the client and is used to assist the thematic analysis of the data for the first research question. Our approach to transcription also acted as a route towards noticing interactionally 'interesting' features/ extracts, to be used in the conversation analysis (Silverman 2017).

We used transcription of the interviews as a key 'noticing device' (ten Have 2007: 97). The Jeffersonian system of symbols we (partially) adopted aims to tread a middle way between a phonetic transcription (accurate, but difficult to read without a great deal of familiarity with the international phonetic alphabet and very consuming of space on the page) and a content-focused transcription (easy to read, but not at all an accurate representation of how the interactants are speaking) (ten Have 2007). The result of this compromise is a style of transcription that, we hope, provides an idea of how the interactants are actually speaking whilst still being fairly readable. There is no rule book for this 'middle way', and different users of Jefferson's system use slightly different sets of symbols or develop new symbols to represent the features of spoken interaction of interest to them; see Appendix A for a list of symbols used in the transcripts of the data collected for this study.

ETHICAL ISSUES

When the interviews that provided the data for this study were recorded by the Centre for Global Education York, ethical issues were not, initially, considered in a way that would be familiar to most academic researchers. In particular, the community project was conducted without obtaining in writing what is usually considered full and informed consent from the participants. At a later stage in the project, when we were invited to work with the interview data, the issue of consent was raised and a consent form developed. The consent forms were discussed with the project participants, taking into account the possibility that some of the informants might not be familiar with the nature of academic practice and the ways in which their data could be used. It was important that, in addition to the forms, a clear verbal explanation was offered to each interviewee to make sure that each individual had fully understood the implications of their consent.

There were a number of risks to explain to the interviewees. Firstly, given the relationship between the project leaders and the participants that had developed in the weeks leading up to the interviews, there was a chance that the participants might have disclosed personal information to the project leaders, which they might later regret or might not wish to share with a wider audience. To guard against this, the project leaders were advised to send a transcript of their interview out to the participants, asking them to confirm that they were happy with the content. As the project involved a number of people holding an immigrant status in the UK, the participants were asked to pay attention to this aspect of their interviews.

The consent form guaranteed the informants' confidentiality, in line with the advice of the British Association for Applied Linguistics (BAAL 2006). Securing informants' anonymity is a common research practice, and it is also expected of the researchers by the Data Protection Act (1998). In this study, several methods of guaranteeing informants' privacy were used. The transcripts were anonymised, and an anonymisation log was created, recording pseudonyms, replacement terms and vague descriptors (including continent, not country, of origin and gender-neutral pronouns). However, due to the collaborative nature of this research, it is important to emphasise that it was not possible to avoid meetings between the researcher, the participants and the Centre for Global Education York project leaders. The balance between collaboration and data protection is not always an easy one to strike for researchers working on community projects. We have taken care in this publication to protect the identities of the project participants, while at the same time providing an opportunity for their stories to be re-created.

In the next chapter, we present the two analyses which were conducted as part of this case study. The chapter begins with the thematic analysis which was carried out in response to the client's needs (research question one). Then, five extracts are presented to illustrate the conversation analysis that we used to explore the interaction between the project leaders and the participants (research question two). The chapter ends with a series of recommendations for interviewers that are based on our findings. Our recommendations are made in the spirit of our problem-solving discipline, applied linguistics: while the thematic analysis appears to present some initial 'findings', the subsequent conversation analysis complicates the meaning of these. Our recommendations aim to raise awareness of how interaction results in new, not found, stories and how interviewees might be allowed the largest possible spaces to create their stories. The problem we uncover in the thematic analysis is that, without a highly developed sensitivity to the ways in which interaction works, stories can be unintentionally constrained by the very project workers who aim to give their participants a voice. The recommendations at the end of this chapter aim to help to solve this problem.

References

Boyatzis, R. E. (1998). *Transforming qualitative information: Thematic analysis and code development*. London: Sage.

Braun, V., & Clarke, V. (2006). Using thematic analysis in psychology. *Qualitative Research in Psychology, 3*(2), 77–101.

Braun, V., & Clarke, V. (2019). Reflecting on reflexive thematic analysis. *Qualitative Research in Sport, Exercise and Health, 11*(4), 589–597.

British Association for Applied Linguistics. (2006). *Recommendations on good practice in applied linguistics.* [Online]. Retrieved February 5, 2019, from www.baal.org.uk/dox/goodpractice_full.pdf.

Centre for Global Education York. (2014). [Online]. Retrieved July 2, 2019, from https://www.theCentreforGlobalEducationYorkork.org.

Data Protection Act. (1998).

Garton, S., & Copland, F. (2010). 'I like this interview; I get cakes and cats!': The effect of prior relationships on interview talk. *Qualitative Research, 10*(5), 533–551.

Gibbs, G. R. (2007). Thematic coding and categorizing. In *Analyzing qualitative data.* London: Sage.

ten Have, P. (1990). *Methodological issues in conversation analysis.* [Online]. Retrieved January 28, 2020, from www.paultenhave.nl/mica.htm.

ten Have, P. (2007). *Doing conversation analysis: A practical guide.* London: Sage.

Jefferson, G. (2004). Glossary of transcript symbols with an introduction. In G. H. Lerner (Ed.), *Conversation analysis: Studies from the first generation.* Amsterdam; Philadelphia: John Benjamins Publishing Company.

Mann, S. (2016). *The research interview: Reflective practice and reflexivity in research processes.* Basingstoke: Palgrave Macmillan.

Robson, C. (2011). *Real world research: A resource for users of social research methods in applied settings.* Chichester, UK: Wiley.

Sacks, H., Schegloff, E., & Jefferson, G. (1974). A simplest systematics for the organization of turn taking for conversation. *Language, 50,* 696–735.

Silverman, D. (2017). How was it for you? The Interview Society and the irresistible rise of the (poorly analyzed) interview. *Qualitative Research, 17*(2), 144–158.

Wetherell, M. (2003). Racism and the analysis of cultural resources in interviews. In H. van den Berg, M. Wetherell, & H. Houtkoop-Steenstra (Eds.), *Analyzing race talk: Multidisciplinary approaches to the interview.* Cambridge: Cambridge University Press.

CHAPTER 4

Analysis and Discussion

Abstract This chapter includes analysis of the interview data and a discussion of the findings. The chapter is organised into two sections to reflect the two different methods of data analysis used in the study: thematic analysis and conversation analysis (CA). The findings of the thematic analysis are reported according to the three themes that were pre-identified by our 'client', the Centre for Global Education York. Five extracts from the interview data, transcribed using CA conventions, are also presented in this chapter, each followed by an analysis of various features of the talk occurring in these extracts.

Keywords Thematic analysis • Conversation analysis • Data extracts • Recommendations

This chapter presents the analysis and discussion of the data that was collected as part of the York's Hidden Stories community project. The chapter is divided into two main parts: thematic analysis and conversation analysis. In part one the results of thematic analysis are presented. The findings of the thematic analysis are reported in three sub-sections according to the three themes identified by the client: (1) reasons for migrating to York, (2) values, (3) barriers. Each sub-section presents a summary of the theme, as well as four illustrative stories about individual participants.

© The Author(s) 2020
R. Wicaksono, D. Zhurauskaya, *York's Hidden Stories*,
https://doi.org/10.1057/978-1-137-55839-8_4

In the second part of this chapter, five extracts, transcribed using conversation analysis conventions, are presented, each followed by an analysis of various features of the talk that occurs in the data. In other words, each extract demonstrates an interesting conversational phenomenon that was noted during the analysis of the whole dataset. The conversation analysis will help to answer research question two: how do the interviewers' contributions shape the interaction with the interviewees?

Thematic Analysis

Three themes were identified by the client as being important and potentially useful in reporting back to the funders of the community project. The three themes were:

- what people say about reasons for migrating to York;
- values and 'treasures' in their lives and how those change as a consequence of coming to York; and
- the barriers people had to overcome when they came to York.

The aim of the York's Hidden Stories project was to capture and share the experiences of York's Black, Asian and Minority Ethnic community. Therefore, it was decided to structure the thematic analysis to allow a selection of participants' stories to be shared with the reader of the project's final report. In each section, below, a summary of what all fifteen participants said on each theme is presented and illustrated with four detailed examples.

The information about immigration status mainly came from the beginning of the interviews. In a few interviews, there were facts about immigration status added at other points in the interview. This information is reported within the thematic analysis.

In the section of the interviews on the topic of values, the interviewees were asked a range of questions about what is important for them. As the interviews were only semi-structured, in almost all instances, the questions were formed slightly differently, or sometimes even omitted, perhaps because the interviewers felt that the question had been covered previously. Here is a summary of the scripted questions, various versions of which were asked in the 'values' section of the interviews:

- Where do you get your values from?
- What do you treasure the most in life?

- Has coming to York changed your values and what you treasure?
- What do you treasure the most about your home country?
- What do you treasure about York?

In the section about barriers, the participants were asked the following questions:

- Are there any barriers you had to overcome in life?
- What helped you to overcome barriers?
- Has living in York created any barriers for you?
- Has living in York helped you to overcome certain barriers?

Although we attempt to report what the participants in the community project said about their experiences of living in York in the summaries provided below, it is important to emphasise the danger of over-generalising from their experiences. The answers given by the participants during the interviews were potentially influenced by a number of factors, for example, the interview context, the pre-existing relationship between participants and interviewers, the participants' confidence in the use of English (the language of the interviews) and the fact that the interviews were recorded. Therefore, it is important to note that the data presented in the thematic analysis is certainly subject to further debate. This aspect of the findings of the thematic analysis will be discussed in more detail in Chap. 5.

Reasons for Coming to York

The participants described a number of different reasons for migrating to York. The main reasons were study, work or to join family. A small number of participants had arrived in York as children, accompanying parents who came to York for work or as refugees. The number of years that the participants had lived in York ranged from seven months to forty-one years. A common theme for all participants was what they perceive to be the characteristic features of York. In particular, they highlighted that they liked York for its historic heritage, security and beauty. One participant commented that York was a 'very traditional society'. These reasons for coming to York are illustrated below, in the stories told by four individual participants and summarised by us.

Diara

Diara came to York as a student in the 1980s. They did not state why they choose York for their studies but they mentioned that the first time they came to York was to visit their sister who was also a student at a local university. After graduation, Diara went back to their town of origin, however, they realised that they really missed York and therefore decided to apply for a job in the city. They said 'my erm my time in York erm sort of developed from being a student (.) to erm (.) loving it so much [...] I really really missed York so much that I decided that I needed to live here'. They explained 'I sent for the local newspapers to be posted to my house every Wednesday when the jobs came out (.) until I got a job in York (.) and I got a job in York and I moved here'. Diara was married and living in York with their partner and three children at the time of the interview.

Jamal

Jamal first arrived in the UK with their family as a refugee from a country in Africa in the 1970s. In their reflection on their immigration experience Jamal said 'we had to leave within three months (.) so we left [name of country], came here in England, penniless, left everything and er (.) stayed in a camp'. Jamal was born into an Asian family who lived in Africa, having established a successful business there. When Jamal and their family first arrived in the UK they stayed in London and then in Lincolnshire before settling in York. Jamal described the reason for their family ending up in York was a result of the UK government decision for refugees to be spread around the country, as opposed to only settling in larger cities. As Jamal said, 'when we were in a camp (.) er the social worker from York came and they said that York is a nice place and you will like it (.) would you like to come with us and look'. When Jamal and their father went to see York they liked it and decided to settle there. Jamal commented 'we've never looked back all the brothers and sister got education here they got their degrees here and then I got married in York and it was the first [name of religion] wedding in York'. At the time of the interview, Jamal was living in York with their partner.

Alex

Alex moved to York with their partner, who is English. At the time of the interview, they had been living in York for ten years and had three children. Alex met their partner in their country of origin in South America where they lived for twelve years before moving to York. In their reflection on the reasons their family came to England, Alex said 'the main point was giving to my children an a better education (.) er thinking this is the best way or the best thing you can leave when you are not with them'. The reason they came to York in particular was because their partner's family lived there. As Alex put it, 'the reason was coming to live very close for [partner's name] family'.

Chima
Chima left their country of origin at the age of twenty-three to come to the UK. Their main reason for coming to York was employment at a local university. At the time of the interview Chima lived in York with their partner and children. Before coming to the UK, Chima studied and worked in Africa, and had also lived in Asia and North America. Chima said that the move to York was not easy as they and their family had an established life in another British city, which they had had to leave behind. However, when they visited York for a job interview, and then showed their family round, they all fell in love with York and its historic features. They commented 'I just felt I am in the right place (.) you know you have got your place and you feel that's where I needed to be now'.

According to the UK Office for National Statistics (ONS) (2014), the main reason immigrants give for coming to the UK is work. Other reasons, in order of frequency, are study, accompanying or joining others, seeking asylum and returning to live in their country of origin. Broadly speaking, the project participants reported the same reasons for coming to York: work, study and accompanying or joining family.

Values

The participants' responses to questions about their values and treasures included the following:

- *Where do you get your values from?*
The majority of participants stated that their values were handed down to them from their parents. Other sources of values were partners, friends, social and political groups and values that were grounded in what the participants described as their 'native' culture, religion and education.

- *What do you treasure the most in life?*
In answer to this question, many participants said that family (children, siblings, parents, spouses) and friends were their greatest treasure. Abstract values that the participants said they treasured included the capacity to

smile, being happy, cooking for friends and family, faith, religion, interest in the origin of, and differences between, people.

- *Has coming to York changed your values and what you treasure?*

This question was a problematic one for a number of the participants, and many answered that they did not know. Some participants said that coming to York had not changed their values and treasures. Others suggested that their values (or at least their ability to express these) had changed, saying, for example: 'It allows me to be who I am'. Other participants said that they didn't know whether their values had changed.

- *What do you treasure the most about your home country?*

The answers to this question varied a great deal and included my grandmother, all my life in the country of origin, the weather, food and music.

- *What do your treasure about York?*

In answer to this question, a few people said that there was nothing that they treasure about York. Some said that they liked the city generally or mentioned specific places within the city that are associated with special memories. Other answers included the Shambles (a famous medieval street in the city), the people of York and the charity shops (where second-hand goods are sold at low prices and proceeds are used to support a charity). Four brief summaries, written by us, of what individual participants said about their values are presented below.

Chardon

Chardon said that a lot of their values came from their own and their family's life experience. When they were little they were separated from their father, as their mother moved to the UK with their English stepfather. When asked about what they value the most in life, Chardon stated, 'the relationship with my dad'. They talked a lot about their father throughout the interview. They also spoke very fondly of their grandmother and mentioned that she was a special person from whom they learned a lot. Their responses suggested that they felt very strongly about the value of education. They emphasised that a lack of 'the opportunity for education' is a major barrier that people from their country of origin face.

Sasha

When Sasha was asked about where they get their values from, they explained that they first of all get their values from the society, parents, and then stressed 'that much influences from friends'. Sasha described their values as 'common Christian values'. Sasha illustrated these values by saying that these are 'common rules for (.) for everyone in [their country of origin]', adding 'yeah it's like common don't kill people don't (.) argue with people and stuff like that (.) yeah (.) just be kind for everyone'. When asked about what they treasured in life Sasha talked about their family, partner, and friends. They went on to explain that their treasures are all about people not objects, 'because objects are always changed (.) around (.) everyone (.) ... but friends (.) parents they always the same (.) will be in your life'. Sasha also mentioned that their values and treasures had not changed as a consequence of coming to the UK.

Bao

When Bao was asked about where they get their values from, they said, 'I get it from my (.) erm (.) mum's behaviour... and I get it from bible (.) and from Church (.) and from watching (.) everyone that's (.) others how they live and how they you know behave'. They also mentioned their mum in response to a question about important experiences, saying 'its not an event (.) it's uh its about my mum'. Referring to the time before they lived in York, Bao said 'I think money was treasure (.) in [country of origin]'. When Bao talked about the difference that moving to York made to their values they said, 'actually I feel er easy er thankful (.) for small things'. They explained that in their country of origin they worked a lot and 'here I have bunch of time to think about myself and (.) er watch how the how other people lived (.) so I think it's changing my beliefs'. Their example of these reflections on others was related to charity and to the charity shops in York, 'here I see (.) they are just uhm happy to give (.) donate (.) and to buy from the charity shop'.

Yun

Yun said that what they valued in life was their family life, in particular their children. They commented that if they were living in their country of origin it would be different, because they would have to live with their parents-in-law and it is common in that society for people to 'have to value father, mother-in-law, father-in-law'. When asked about what Yun treasured about York, they replied 'you can get more facility' and 'you can make your own choice'.

Barriers

The interview questions about 'barriers' and a summary of the participants' answers are as follows:

- *Are there any barriers you had to overcome in life?*

Participants mentioned being accepted by their partner's family, being
mixed race in the 80s, difference, lack of confidence, gender discrimination in the workplace, poverty, divorce, getting an education, missing their
country of origin, themselves, racism, settling down, language, limitations
to travel and perfectionism.

- *What helped you to overcome barriers?*

The participants mentioned that the following had helped them to
overcome the barriers they had faced in their lives: being nice to people,
attending courses with a focus on confidence building, reflection, faith,
being determined and 'myself'.

- *Has living in York created any barriers for you?*

The majority of the participants said that York did not create any barriers for them. However, some shared that they found it hard living away
from their families and felt pressure from their cultural community in
the city.

- *Has living in York helped you to overcome certain barriers?*

Some participants stated that nothing changed for them as a consequence of coming to York. A few participants mentioned that in York they
were able to have more rights and justice than in their countries of origin.
Four brief summaries of what individual participants said about the barriers they have faced are presented below.

Zenith

*Zenith described their main barrier in their country of origin as poverty.
After they lost their father, their family struggled a lot financially. This also
affected Zenith's schooling. However, with the help of their grandmother, who
was very encouraging, they were able to gain confidence and do well in life. A
barrier, Zenith mentioned in their interview is the divorce proceedings
between them and their partner, which were ongoing. As a result of this process, Zenith said that they were not able to see their child who was living with*

their ex-partner. They also said that 'seeing er a child being you know er unfairly treated by their parents and actually actually used by the system again and you know legally that I can't you know discuss it'.

Andri

When asked about the barriers that Andri had to overcome in life, they replied that currently they saw language as a barrier. They made a direct link between their linguistic abilities and self-confidence, saying that 'it makes you less self-confident'. They commented that 'if I speak it [English] better, I would be more (.) I would be more integrated into society; I would be more part of the community here'. Another obstacle that Andri described was that they were restricted to traveling to other countries as they needed visas for most countries in the world. They commented, 'it really restricts me because I want to travel'. Andri's frustrations with travel are reinforced because they saw that there are a lot of cheap travel deals that are promoted in the UK, however, for them, the need to obtain a visa is a big obstacle to taking advantage of these deals.

Sage

The main barrier that Sage stated that they had to overcome in life was being shy as a child. They also said that these confidence issues had been a barrier growing up and that it took them a lot of courage to overcome this barrier. They described a critical moment when one day they decided to make an effort to overcome being a timid person. Sage said: 'I got so, so sick of it that, that I remember just saying to my friend, you know, I'm not gonna be shy anymore and I just (.) said to her and she was like, okay (laughs) and from that point I remember making such a big effort to not be shy'. Another barrier that Sage described was that they sometimes felt too comfortable living in York. They reflected that their formal education took place in York, their family lived in York and that they really liked York and what it had to offer.

Chris

Chris shared that the main barrier that they had to overcome in life was limited access to education; specifically, 'an education that would change my life and the life of my family members and the community at large'. Chris reported that, traditionally, in their community of origin the priority for education is given to male members of the family. Therefore, as a young child, born into a polygamous family, they had to persuade their father to educate them. Chris shared their own experience of being different and arriving in a new community. They said that when they first came to York it was very rare to see a person of colour on the streets, but when they did see someone they felt like 'running after them and telling them talk to me'. They described a situation in which a stranger in the street who was eavesdropping on a conversation they were having with their friend asked them to speak in English, 'because they were in England'. They said that they struggled a lot to accept this type of attitude. Chris also said that sometimes they found that people asked questions or negatively commented about their culture of origin, for example about rituals which were common in their culture of origin, but which are unusual in the UK. Coming to live in York gave Chris an opportunity for education as they got a scholarship to study at a local university. However, it also created a barrier in that they missed their place of origin and felt that they were not able to emotionally support their family through hard times. Chris commented 'sometimes being away from home can be quite daunting'.

The barriers experienced by the project participants in York ranged from feeling lonely and missing their country of origin to prejudice from their own cultural communities and racism on the streets of York. The problem of racism in York was also described by Craig et al. (2010) who called for key people and agencies in York to strengthen their commitment to racial equality and to actively combat racism. The Craig report highlights how some individuals they surveyed were experiencing loneliness and cultural isolation, experiences which sometimes led to nervous breakdowns and depression (Craig et al. 2010). The report states that 'it remains the case that some of the minority ethnic groups continue to feel a sense of cultural dislocation and isolation and have argued for the need for specific facilities to enable their group to become more visible' (2010: 17), findings that are supported by our thematic analysis.

Conclusion

The responses to research question one are summarised below:

- *What themes occur in the interviews with York's Black, Asian and Minority Ethnic residents on the topics identified by the client (i.e. reasons for migration, values and barriers)?*

The main reasons for coming to York stated by the project participants were study, work or joining family. A small number of participants had arrived in York as children, accompanying parents who came to York for work or as refugees. The participants' values were expressed using the following words: respect, family, friends, loyalty, honesty, generosity, difference, education, faith and community. When asked about barriers in their lives, the participants stated the following: being accepted by spouse's family, being mixed race in the 80s, difference, lack of confidence, gender discrimination at workplace, poverty, poverty mentality, divorce, prejudice from their own community, getting an education, missing 'home', 'myself', racism, settling down, language, limitations to travel and perfectionism.

Generalisations about data, without careful consideration of the discursive context in which it was collected, should be made with extreme caution. In all cases, the 'findings' reported above occurred in the context of a question from an interviewer and, in some cases, in the context of a follow-up question or a summarised answer. The conversation analysis presented below will illustrate in more depth some of the ways in which the 'findings' of the thematic analysis were in fact co-creations, constructed in interaction by the interviewers and their interviewees.

CONVERSATION ANALYSIS

In the five extracts selected from the data and shown below, the interview participants are referred to as IR1/IR2 (interviewers) and IE (interviewee). There were two interviewers present at each interview, but not all the extracts have both of them interacting with interviewees. Each extract begins with a description of the topic in the extract, followed by analysis, and recommendations for community project interviewers to consider when preparing for, and conducting, their interviews.

Extract 1

In the section of the interview from which this extract is taken, the IR is asking the IE questions about the values and treasures that they had. The extract relates to the last question in that section, before the IR moves onto another topic. Extract 1 begins with the IR summarising prior talk before asking a question in line 9.

IR: Interviewer
IE: Interviewee

```
01 IR:    so you (.) er (.) when you describe [country] then (.) obviously (1.0)
02        the thing tha:t (.) you treasure most is >obviously< your dad that you
03        left behind [the:re]
04 IE:                [yeah]
05 IR:    when you think of thi:s country then (2.0) am I getting an
06        inkling that you treasure the opportunities
07 IE:    yeah
08        (1.0)
09 IR:    I mean is there anything else that you treasure about
10        the UK then
11        (.)
12 IE:    (lip-smack).hh erm (2.0) (lip-smack) what do I treasure about
13        the UK?=
14 IR:    =or even York perhaps (.) is there something about
15        living in York=
16 IE:    =yes (.) I actually (.) really love (.) living in York now (.)
17        again when I first came to York I thou:ght it was one of the
18        most bo:ring cities
19        ((laughter))
20 IE:    a:nd=
21 IR:    =so what age where you when you came to York then
22 IE:    I wa:s (.) round about (.) thirteen fourteen
23 IR:    ok
24 IE:    (.) yes a:nd (.) one of the first things that you notice of
25        somebody of colour erm (.) is (.) of course=
26 IR:    =a rarity
27 IE:    yeah (.) [and]
28 IR:             [yeah]
29 IE:    here wasn't much hehe
30 IR:    okay
31 IE:    e:m (.) so: it was another (.) moment of (1.0) ((sigh)) hh just
32        (.) being kind of (.) on your own again (.) you know (.) e:rm
33        (.) a::nd (.) >it was a struggle< but ((lip-smack)) I think
34        those experiences sort of made me (1.0) e:rm (1.0) what's the
35        word (1.0) stronger in a lot of ways
36 IR:    so they give you character
37 IE:    erm (0.5) it did
```

The talk prior to this extract consisted of an extended exchange of short questions and answers by the IR and IE. The above extract begins with the IR launching a new topic, which is indicated by a discourse marker *so* in line 1. The discourse marker 'so' is commonly used to express inferential connections; however, Bolden (2009) argues that this marker is also a useful discourse tool for prefacing sequence-initiated actions such as questions. In particular, as we see in the above extract, it indicates to the listener that the upcoming talk is not related to the previous sequences and the speaker is introducing a new topic. It could be argued that the interviewer is using the discourse marker 'so' to advance their interactional agenda.

After a small pause and a hesitation sound, the IR begins to summarise the prior talk in lines 1–3 and 5–6. In line 4 the IE produces a minimal response token *yeah* to indicate that they are listening and in line 7 is using the same token to agree with the IR's formulation. The IR pauses in line 8 creating a possible transition relevance place, a moment in which either speaker can self-select to talk, providing an opportunity for the IE to add to their previous affirmative answer in line 7. No elaboration follows so the IR self-selects a turn in lines 9–10 with a further question *I mean is there anything else that you treasure about the UK then?*. Fox Tree and Schrock (2002) suggest that one of the uses of the discourse marker 'I mean' is to indicate an upcoming adjustment. Therefore, it is possible to argue that what happens in lines 9 and 10 is the IR reformulating the request for clarification that was produced earlier in lines 5–6.

There is another pause in line 11, and line 12 begins with the IE taking time to think by producing a lip-smack, a hesitation marker *.hh erm*, followed by a two-second pause, another lip-smack and a restatement of the question: *what do I treasure about the UK?*. The IR interprets this hesitation as lack of further answers from the IE and in line 14 offers an alternative question *or even York perhaps* and after a micro pause adds *is there something about living in York*. What is interesting to note here is that the IR changes *anything else* in the original question to *something* in the second version. It could be suggested that the IR redesigned the polarity of the question in order to achieve an aligning response. Heritage and Robinson (2011) suggest that questions which use 'anything else' are more likely to get a grammatically preferred negative response, whereas questions that use 'something' are more likely to result in a positive response.

A positive response comes immediately in line 16, followed by a further elaboration in lines 16–18. This response provokes a burst of laughter in line 19. It has been noted that IE-initiated laughter occurs less frequently in interviews compared to IR-initiated laugher (Hak 2003). It may be that the reason why IE-initiated laughter happens in line 19 is to justify the statement in lines 17–18 that *York...it was one of the most boring cities*. It has been observed that IE-initiated laughter is an interactional move can create a sense of intimacy (Jefferson et al. 1987). By sharing that *York is a boring city*, followed by laughter, the respondent conveys something that cannot be shared with just anyone, an 'in-group' move which functions as a kind of potential bonding activity. Hak (2003: 210) notes that 'teller's laughter marks the told even as "improper" and at the same time, demonstrates that the teller knows this'. The IR does not self-select to take a turn in response to IE-initiated laugher, and line 20 is taken by the IE with an elongated *a:nd*. However, the IR interrupts this turn with a new question in line 21.

The exchange that happens in lines 16–35 is an interesting example of an extreme case formulation (Pomerantz 1986), which is used by the IE as a way of legitimising their claim in line 16. In answer to the IR question is *there something [that you treasure] about living in York* the IE responds in line 16 with *yes (.) I actually (.) really love (.) living in York now*. The IE goes on to talk about how negative their experience of living in York was in the past, by saying things like *it was one of the most boring cities; things that you notice of somebody of colour… there wasn't much; it was a struggle.* It could be argued that the effect of the extreme formulation of *I actually (.) really love (.) living in York now* defends the IE against potential challenges to the legitimacy of the experiences that they goes on to talk about. In other words, this formulation is allowing them to talk about their negative experiences, in response to what was invited to be an account of a treasured memory

The IE responds in line 22. What happens in lines 24–25 may be a continuation of line 20, where the IE was not given the opportunity to carry on talking. An interruption happens again in line 26, however this time with a word suggested by the IR: *rarity*. The IE agrees and carries on talking about this new topic in lines 29 and 31–35. The extract ends with the IR providing a closing statement, which the IE agrees with in line 37.

Two different types of contributions made by the IR can be observed in the extract above. Firstly, dropping an unsuccessful question and rephrasing, choosing a narrower topic, that is, asking about York instead of the UK. This means that the question in line 9 remains unanswered and the only possible answer, which makes a contribution to the thematic analysis, is the interaction in lines 5–6, where the IE confirms the IR's assumption that *opportunities* are what the IE treasures. Secondly, what might be seen as helping the IE to find the right word in line 26 is actually constraining the IE's subsequent talk. The fact that the IR breaks the IE's turn by suggesting the world *rarity* is most likely not accidental. It is possible to argue that the effect of these moves by the IR is to project the kind of information they want to hear more about. In this case, it is also possible that the IR is confirming that it is acceptable to talk about what some might see as a sensitive topic.

Recommendation

The extract above demonstrates how interviewers can make a contribution to their interviewees' responses. Our recommendation, therefore, is that if an interviewer notices that they have made a specific contribution, such as offering a word that has narrowed the range of choices that the interviewee was presented with, they can consider following it up with a more general contribution, such as, 'is there something else you want to say?' or 'do you have some more comments about this topic?'.

Extract 2

Extract 2 was taken from the beginning of the interview. The question that appeared prior to the one in the extract below was about how moving to the UK changed the IE's values and treasures. The extract below starts with a new question about what the IE really treasures about their country of origin.

IR: Interviewer
IE: Interviewee

```
01 IR:   is there anything (.) in particular that y:ou (.) really do
02        treasure about [country] °then°
03        (2.0)
04 IE:    any particular
05 IR:    anything (.) you know it could be foo:d music (.) [people]
06 IE:                                                      [Y:ES] (.)
07        yes I love the music
08 IR:    mm
09        (0.2)
10 IE:    and er (.) is here I miss that music (.) I do when I
11        play in the car my children don't like it [((laughter))]
12 IR:                                               [right]
13 IE:    oh [parent] put English one on ((laughter))
14 IR:    right yeah
15 IE:    so I miss (.) but I do I miss it but (.) °yeah°
16 IR:    (.) so what do you treasure about living in York then
```

In the extract above, the IR begins a turn with a question is there anything (.) in particular that y:ou (.) really do treasure about [country]

°then°. What can be noted in lines 1–2 is that the IR is inviting the IE to think of any answer by saying the word *anything*; however, it is followed by an invitation to think of something specific by placing an the emphasis on *in particular* and the two pauses, which add further emphasis. In line 3, there is a significant pause before a request for clarification from the IE follows in line 4 with a repair initiator *any particular*. In line 5, the IR replies with *anything* which is followed by a pause. The pause is a potential transition relevance place that provides an opportunity for the IE to proceed with a reply. However, it is a very short pause, and as the IE is silent, the IR carries on with a list of candidates for *anything* by suggesting *you know it could be foo:d music (.) [people]*. In line 6, the IE begins a turn with an overlap *[Y:ES] (.) yes I love the music*, selecting *music* from the list offered by the IR in the previous turn. In lines 8 and 9, there is an acknowledgement token *mm* and a pause, which are interpreted by the IE as an invitation to continue their turn in line 10. It starts with a hesitation but elicits more details as the IE continues talking in lines 10–15 with the help of backchanneling tokens such as 'right' and 'yeah' in lines 12 and 14 from the IR to indicate active listening. Back channelling (also known as response tokens; see Gardner 2001; Peters and Wong 2015) is a very useful technique for interviewers to use to encourage more detailed answers. The extract ends with the IR's next question.

In the extract above, we observe how the IR's contribution in line 5, which may have been an attempt to clarify a problem for the IE, influences the IE's choice of topic. If we considered the exchange in lines 1–5 in the context of everyday interaction, it could be argued that providing a list of words is a useful strategy, likely to be successful in explaining what is meant by *anything*. Furthermore, in a reflective vignette featured in Steve Mann's book (2016: 25), one researcher comments on his own use of a 'complex, multi-layered question' as providing the interviewee with more interactional resources to respond to and more thinking time. Research on elaborate questions in focus groups also suggests that participants may find it helpful to be provided with multiple alternative suggestions to respond to (Puchta and Potter 1999). However, Puchta and Potter (1999) highlight that the use of elaborate questions in focus groups is a very organised strategy of eliciting desired answers. Arguably, in an interview situation, this particular strategy could be less useful, perhaps even undermining of the validity of a subsequent thematic analysis of the IE's responses. Therefore, this extract is another example of the potential constraining effect the IR's contribution might have on the IE talk. It illustrates a different type of constraining from the one seen in the first extract, which is achieved by offering a list of candidate suggestions. In this extract, the trigger of the constraining contribution also differs; it is after the IE asks for a clarification in line 4 *any particular* that the IR provides a list of possible answers. It could be argued that in line 4, the IE could have been pausing for thought. However, it was interpreted by the IR as indicating a need for clarification, and an explanation followed.

In line 13 we see the IE using direct reported speech *oh [parent] put English one on ((laughter))* to describe that their children ask them to change music in the car. Coulmas (1986) outlines that direct reported speech recalls on the original utterance by claiming the exact words used by the initial speaker. Here the IE is using the words *oh [parent]* to indicate that it is their children's talk that is being reported. The use of a turn initial 'oh', also referred to as 'change-of-state-token' by Heritage (1984), at the beginning of line 13 announces a shift from IE own speech to one said by their children. Holt (1996: 228) argues that direct reported speech is often used to 'provide evidence that supports the speaker's version of an event'. In case of this extract, it is possible to argue that the IE is using the direct reported speech to support their statement in line 11 that their children don't like them playing the music from their country of origin in the car. Holt (2017) also argues that speakers use direct reported speech to engage the listener in storytelling.

What happens in line 13 can also be described as an example of 'conversationalisation' in the interviewee's utterance. Conversationalisation is described by Lee (2003: 58) as a local discursive practice where an interviewee incorporates someone else's voice into their response. Such utterances are usually initiated by respondents with discourse markers 'oh', 'sure', 'OK' and 'yeah'. Often those discourse markers are used to indicate the speaker's response to a previous turn by another speaker. However, Lee (2003) shows data extracts where the above discourse markers are responses to a hypothetical turn by a constructed interlocutor. This is also observed in line 13 of the above extract which starts with *oh [parent] put English one on ((laughter))*, where *oh* marks a transition to the interviewee's child's voice. The oh-prefaced response enables the interviewee to elaborate their view and also to suggest that their opinion was formed taking opposing views into account, making their response sound more credible. Lee (2003) demonstrates how interviewees use what he calls conversationalisation in order to compensate for the constraints imposed by the role of an interviewer. Interviewees are aware that an interviewer can't resort to ordinary conversation, hence why they make use of conversationalisation to covertly enable the interviewers to engage in the conversation, 'but with the benefit that this engagement is subject to their control' (Lee 2003: 60).

Recommendation

Based on this extract, something for an interviewer to consider is how to remain general when explaining something broad. A possible recommendation in this case could be: if an interviewer notices that an interviewee problematises their question, an interviewer could consider replying with 'yes' or 'anything' followed by a pause. In this way, an interviewer can avoid adding more information to the original question and, instead, attempt to simply confirm that the interviewee has understood the question as was intended. Alternatively, if an interviewer chooses to use elaborate questions, they have to be aware that such strategy might elicit answers tailored to the interview agenda.

Extract 3

The extract below appears in the section with questions about values and treasures. Prior to this extract, the interviewee was asked about where they get their values from. Extract 3 begins with the interviewer asking the interviewee a question about what they treasure in life.

IR1: Interviewer
IR2: Second interviewer
IE: Interviewee

```
01 IR1:  .hh and when we think about you know these values (2.0) if we
02       thought about treasures then in life: (1.0) give me some
03       things that you really treasure in life then
04 IE:   (2.0) °tre:asu:re° (.)
06 IR1:  °mmm°
07       (2.0)
08 IE:   I think every day is treasure (.)
09 IR1:  °wow°=
10 IE:   =but sometimes I have bad days (.)
11 IR1:  [((lip-smack)) okay]
12 IE:   [but] hehe ((smiley voice)) usually I uhm (.) when I wake up I
13       try to: pray (.)
14 IR1:  mmm
15 IE:   for the (.) everything
```

```
16 IR1:   mmm
17 IE:    that I a:m (.) happy (.)
18 IR1:   mmm
19 IE:    and I have good life (2.0) °a::nd° (.) >yeah<
20 IR1:   so that sets your days then the day (1.0) ahead (.) you
21        hopefully it's [something]
22 IE:                   [yeah]
23 IR1:   that you will treasure
24 IR2:   °yeah°
25 IE:    okay so life is important to you as well then (1.0) do you
26        thi:nk (.) coming to: here (.) in the UK (.) and
27        >obviously< you're looking at (.) people's behaviour as well
28        (1.5) do you think being in York (.) has changed or moved
29        your values at all (.) and what you treasure
```

The extract above begins with the IR asking a question about what the IE treasures in life. In line 1, the IR begins with an invitation to think about values that were discussed earlier in the interview; however, after a two-second pause, the IR rephrases the invitation to *if we thought about treasures then in life*. This is followed by an explicit request to provide examples of what the IE treasures. It is interesting to note the use of the collective pronoun *we* in line 1 inviting the IE to jointly think about the topic. In using *we*, the IR projects an image of being an equal participant in the interview. However, in line 2 the IR adjusts to the use of a personal pronoun *me* in the request for information, making it into an imperative sentence.

After a long pause in line 4, the IE produces the elongated word °*tre:asu:re*° in a quiet voice, indicating to the IR acceptance of the topic and allowing for some thinking time. After a pause, the IE responds with, *I think every day is treasure*, in line 8. This response is immediately followed by the IR with an interjection—°*wow*°. Research on interjections, including 'wow', suggests that they carry multiple linguistic propositions and have an illocutionary purpose (Ameka 1992; Wierzbicka 1992; Wilkins 1992; Cruz 2009). Wilkins (1992: 151), for example, argues that the 'illocutionary purpose of saying "wow!" is to show how surprised and impressed the speaker is feeling at the moment of speaking'. In the case of this extract, *wow* is followed by the IE's downgrading of their response in line 10 to *but sometimes I have bad days*, potentially (though not necessarily) contradicting their original claim in line 8. What we see in line 12 could be an attempt by the IR to explain the apparent contradiction with a conjunction *but* and laughter. The IE continues in lines 12 and 13 with *usually I uhm (.) when I wake up I try to: pray*.

Lines 14, 16 and 18 consist of the IR's minimal responses, *mmm*, which seem to serve the purpose of continuers (Schegloff 1982). These continuers are produced while the IE is saying, *usually I uhm (.) when I wake up I try to: pray, mmm, for the (.) everything, mmm, that I a:m (.) happy (.) mmm, and I have a good life.* At the end of line 19, after a two-second pause, the IE holds the turn with an elongated *a::nd,* and then, after a short pause, the IE's turn ends with a quick *yeah.* In line 20, the IR presents a formulation, which is a summary of the information produced earlier by the IE (Heritage and Watson 1979). It is possible to state that the extended formulation in the extract above is doing three things. Firstly, it displays the IR's understanding of the IE's prior talk. Secondly, it rephrases the IE's answer to fit better within the IR's question, making it sound like a more newsworthy statement. Finally, it closes the sequence in line 25 with, *okey so life is important to you as well then.* This closing statement is hard to disagree with, and, in the case of this extract, it leaves the IE with nothing to say. After a pause in line 25, which was an opportunity for the IE to comment on the formulation, the IR initiates a new sequence by asking a new question in subsequent lines.

It is interesting to observe three specific contributions in the above extract that are made by the IR. Firstly, the use of the collective and individual pronouns *we* and *me.* This contribution helps the interviewer to manage their role and the power dynamics in the interview situation. Secondly, it can be argued that the interjection in line 9 incorporates a value judgement which encourages the IE to reframe their subsequent talk. Finally, in the last turn of this sequence, the IR uses a formulation to close the topic. This is a useful technique that helps to structure the interview talk, indicating to the IE that a new topic will follow. It also potentially allows for the possibility for the IE to disagree with the formulation.

Recommendation
If an interviewer notices that their contribution was judgemental or changed the direction of an answer, they could try repeating the original question. This, of course, could result in the IE feeling the need to change their answer, if there appears to the IE to be no other warrant for the repetition other than the possibility that their first answer was unsatisfactory. It may be that, once a value judgement has been made by the IR and resulted in a change of course by the IE, all that the IR can do is to disregard the IE's answer. Or to see the answer not as 'content' but as discourse; that is, as evidence of how the IE responds to being contradicted/

disagreed with/judged. It is undoubtable extremely hard to notice one's own language features in the moments of interaction; however, we suggest that researchers and interviewers engage in raising their interview awareness to develop such skills.

Extract 4

The extract below is different from the previous extracts in that it has contributions from both of the IRs. The extract begins with a turn by IR1 that consists of a number of repairs in an attempt to ask a question about what the IE treasures in life.

IR1: Interviewer 1
IR2: Interviewer 2
IE: Interviewee

```
01 IR1:  I:f yo:u had something (.) that yo::u (.) I mean could you
02       share something about (.) something that you truly treasure
03       (1.0) in life (.) is there anythin- I MEAN IT could be
04       something quite physical (.) it could be some (.)  e::r- you
05       know an encounter it could be >anything< something that
06       yo:u've experienced that you re:ally treasure and you're so
07       glad that it's been part of your life
08 IE:   ok.hay:.
09       (8.0)
10 IR1:  just think I me:an the big thing as well i:s you know (.)
11       where you are no:w (.) >it's a number of years< (.) so it
12       might be something that (.) it could be linked to chi:ldhood
13       (.) it could be your tee:nage years (.) it could be (.)
14 IE:   something that I [found on my own]
15 IR1:                   [yes]=
16 IE:   =and it's very important for me=
17 IR1:  = yeah it's something somebody could have given to yo:u as
18       well(.) or you found it or it could have been given as we:ll
19       (2.0)
20 IR2:  I mean (.) it doesn't- it could be a material thing (.) it
21       could also be an idea it could also [be a way]=
22 IR1:                                       [ok]
23 IR2:  = of being [or] =
24 IE:              [mmm]
25 IR2:  = it could be a person you see so there's a lot (.) that for
26       yo:u that is very precious (.) something that is
27       °very very precious°
28       (2.0)
29 IE:   I mean (.) okay (3.0) the thing that I like with myself (1.0)
30       and it's very important for me is like I'm always like very
```

```
31        happy person (.) >I mean< of course I have downs and ups as
32        usual (.) and >things is that< moreover >this you know< I try
33        to: get to know the o:ther people (.) I mean not o:ther in
34        terms of ((smiley voice)) other but you know the people from
35        different cu:ltures (.) it doesn't mean that people of here
36        (.) you know for example I will do some research or I was- you
37        know er (1.0) dealing with other people in [country] like (.)
38        the people that I I could never (0.5) you know met (0.5) for
39        example some drug dealers I was researching like (1.0) or
40        other so many different groups that I could never be in the
41        same room (.) you know (.) and I like you know because (2.0)
42        I'm very easy going in terms of you know (1.0) you know (.)
43        e::u connecting to the people that (.) they do not look like
44        °me° (1.0) and I I feel that (.) you know (1.5) e::r (.) hhhh
45        those are the people who teach me the most of the things
46        in the life (2.0) °I mean° (.) okay I mean I I always I'm
47        always with the people who are from academia (.) like (.) er
48        middle-class people or something okay I'm fine with the
49        friends but (1.0) ( ) the point of view you all just look
50        like each other and just similar you know like sheep (1.0)
51 IR1:   mmm (.)
52 IE:    But when when we have contact with the other people like the
53        the other might be in terms of anything you know but basically
54        >>for example<< cla::ss (.) you know (1.0) ((lip-smack)) >for
55        example< I was working with slum people and I I
56        lived them for- I lived with them for three mo:nths (.) last
57        year (.) a:nd this three months like a thirty year (.) years
58        for me in terms of learning
59 IR1:   mmm
60 IE:    more about the life itself
61 IR1:   mm (1.5) yea that's- thats something very- .hh ye::ah I think
62        that's quite special actually so the value of difference
63        actually and [appreciating that]
64 IE:                 [Exactly (.) Exactly]
65 IR1:   a:nd actually you can learn
```

The above extract begins with the IR1 asking what the IE treasures in
life. The IR1's turn in lines 1–7 consists of a series of self-repairs in repeated
attempts to construct a question that satisfies the IR1. Within this turn the
IR1 changes the extent of the question from, *something that you truly
(1.0) treasure in life* in lines 2–3 to, *something that yo:u've experienced that
you re:ally treasure* in lines 5–6. This lexical change narrows the topic from
a generic *something* to a more specific *something that yo:u've experienced*. In
line 8, the IE replies with an elongated *ok.hay:.* which is produced on an
out-breath with falling intonation, signalling that the IE has understood
the question. However, after a long pause of eight seconds in line 9, the
IR1 launches a new turn, inviting the IE to think about other aspects of
the topic of treasures in life. Furthermore, in line 20, the second

interviewer joins in, providing further prompts for the IE to consider. Together both IRs produce the following list of possible considerations:

Something quite physical
An encounter
Anything
Something that you've experienced
Something that is linked with childhood or teenage years
Something somebody could have given you or you found on your own
A material thing
An idea
A way of being
A person

This list is summarised by the IR2 in line 25 with, *you see so there's a lot*. The extract above demonstrates that the interviewers' questions involved a great deal of repetition. Edmondson and House (1991) describe this as 'the waffle phenomenon'. A possible effect of interviewer's waffling is a potentially overpowering list of considerations presented to the IE in an attempt to help. The downside of all of these suggestions is that it could distract the IE from thinking about their own answer and resorting to choosing an answer from a possible list of considerations made by the IRs.

Let us now consider the answer that this cascade of questions elicited in the above extract. The answer comes in lines 29–58 where the IE provides a reply which consists of a number of statements about the IE. The IE talks about their positive feelings about their perception of themselves as a very happy person (line 31), that they try to get to know other people (line 33) and that they are easy going (line 42). The IE also provides two examples in which they describe their experience of working and living with different social groups, and they state that those experiences have taught them the most in life (lines 52–58). So if we match the IE's answers to the IR's list of considerations, it could be argued that the answers were driven by the IR's suggestions; in particular 'way of being' was described as being a happy person and easy going, and 'encounter' and 'experiences' were reported as trying to get to know other people and an example of working with a particular socio-economic groups.

The extract above ends with the IR1 summarising IE's answer in lines 61–63 and line 65 with an utterance prefaced by a discourse marker 'so' to indicate the recap. In those lines the IR1 says *so the value of difference actually and [appreciating that] ...a:nd actually you can learn*. The sequence ends with the IR formulating a statement that is perhaps more closely aligned with the original question, *in particular could you share something about (.) something that you truly treasure (1.0) in life* (lines 1–3)—the answer is *so the value of difference actually and [appreciating that], [Exactly (.) Exactly] a:nd actually you can learn* (lines 62–65).

What is also notable in the extract above is the eight-second pause in line 9, which arguably is a critical point in this extract. It was interpreted by the IRs as a trigger to elaborate on the original question by providing prompts for the IE to consider. However, it is possible to argue that the interactional work done by the IRs from lines 10 to 27 might not have been necessary, had they given more time for the IE to respond in line 9. Rapley (2001: 312) suggests that an 'IR's silence can work to promote an elaborate answer'. Further research on silence in the classroom provides evidence to show that there is a relationship between silence and more detailed and complex answers from students (Cotton 1988; Rowe 1987; Stahl 1994; Tama 1989). By leaving longer pauses after a question, teachers give time for students to think. This is known as 'think time', the period of silence following a question and ending with a response (Stahl 1994). The same think time phenomenon may also be useful in interviews.

Recommendation

Therefore, a recommendation that could be made here is for interviewers to allow longer silences which will allow time for the interviewees to think of answers. This can potentially lead to more detailed and interesting answers, avoiding further suggestions from interviewers.

Extract 5

The extract below demonstrates an exchange that appears towards the end of an interview and is about barriers that people in the interviewee's country of origin face. As in most of the extracts, the extract below begins with the interviewer asking a question.

IR: Interviewer
IE: Interviewee

```
01 IR:   when you look at your- (.) your home country (.) at [country]
02       (.) and you look at the people in general and the way they live
03       (.) .hh (0.5) e:rm (.) what barriers do you (0.5) do you see
04       that they've got to overcome↓ (.) what are the barriers (.) I
```

```
05          MEAN you mentioned education= [(     )]
06  IE:                                   [=Yeah (.) yeah (.)]
07          definitely (0.5) .hhhh e::rm (.) that's a huge barrier (1.0)
08          ((lip smack)) e:::rm
09          (0.4)
10  IR:     any other barrier
11          (8.0)
12  IE:     mmmm ((lip smack)).hh (0.4) hh it's- it all comes down to
13          education [really]
14  IR:              [yeah]
15          (0.2)
16  IE:     it really does=
17  IR:     =it also the fact that you were saying (.) you know (.) it .hh
18          (0.6) you know hhhhh (.) the main pre- one of the main
19          preoccupations fo::r (0.2) people (.) who (.) are not (0.5)
20          wealthy is to put a meal together (0.5)
21  IE:     hmmmm=
22  IR:     =so:
23          (0.2)
24  IE:     hmmm
25          (0.5)
26  IE:     to- to put a meal together? is that [>what I said<]
27  IR:                                         [ye:ah] to put food on the
28          table
29  IE:     hmm (0.3) hmm (0.2) it is
30          (0.2)
31  IR:     °so° (0.2) so the- (.) there must be (0.5) erm (0.5) barriers
32          there (.) obstacles there (2.0) to prevent people from (.) NOT
33          having (.) you know
34  IE:     yeah
35  IR:     having this as a preoccupation
36          (0.3)
37  IE:     yeah (.) e:rm (1.5) a lot of people are just hh ((sigh))
38          aren't working so .hh (2.0) [yeah]
39  IR:                                 [a lot of people are not working]
40          (0.5)
41  IE:     ((lip smack)) they have to find other ways (.) basically
42          (1.0) e:rm e:rm a:nd those other ways may not be legal (1.0)
43          e::rm (.) so then they (0.7)obviously (0.5) put themselves in
44          danger of getting into trouble another way (.) so:: (.) it's
45          just one thing on top really (0.2) e:rm (2.5) but I think (.)
46          definitely the opportunity for education (0.7) there is a big
47          thing (0.2) e::rm
```

Extract 5 begins with the IR asking a question about barriers that people face in the IE's country of origin. The IR constructs an extended question starting with 'setting the scene' in lines 1 and 2. Such extended question sequences have been noticed (Gardner 2004; Wicaksono 2012) in talk between so-called native and non-native speakers; a question is asked by the native speaker, and then, after leaving a gap for an answer and receiving none, or after no gap at all, the same speaker expands or provides an alternative version of the original question. In Extract 5, the actual question comes (after the setting the scene) in lines 3 and 4, when the IR asks *what barriers do you (0.5) see they've got to overcome.* The IR subsequently pauses and adds, *what are the barriers.* After another short pause in line 4, the IR says *I MEAN you mentioned education.* As in the previous extracts, the IR made a contribution to the IE's answer by offering a possible topic. Let us see how the IE's response unfolds.

In line 6, the IE immediately agrees with two yeah answers, which are also reinforced in line 7 with *definitely.* After a half-a-second pause and a hesitation, the IE strengthens their answer by stating *that's a huge barrier.* The one-second pause at the end of line 7 is a possible transition relevance place for the IR to launch into the next question. However, when the IR does not ask another question, the IE indicates with a hesitation *e:::rm* that they have come to the end of their reply. After another pause in line 9, the IR asks with falling intonation, *any other barrier.* There is a very long pause of eight seconds in line 11 before the IE replies. The response in lines 12–13 is similar to the original response in lines 6–7; the IE produces an elongated *mmmm* sound, lip-smack, in-breaths, out-breaths and pauses, which seem to be an indication that they are struggling to think of another answer. In line 16, the IE tries to close the topic by insisting that it really does come down to education. However, the IR insists on eliciting more on the topic of barriers (lines 17–20). In line 17, the IR says, *you were saying(.) you know,* a similar strategy to line 5, where the IR says *I MEAN you mentioned.* It seems that what the IR is trying to do is to indicate (lines 22–35) to the IE that the responses to the question about barriers have already featured in the interview and what the IR wants is for the IE to restate those answers now. However, the IE remains committed to the original response that *it all comes down to education* and restates this response in lines 46–47.

What we see in Extract 5 is how the IR restates a matter previously mentioned by the IE, which is relevant in response to the question. This might be a useful technique in that it shows that the IR was listening and is aware that the topic was already covered by the IE. If asking questions reinforces the identity of 'interviewer' (assuming that, as we said in Chap. 1, recognition of the interview format is widespread), extended/repeated questions are 'proof' of the interviewer's 'right' to probe and, assuming a 'romantic' conceptualisation of interviews, to really get to the 'heart' of the interviewee's experiences. The extended and repeated questions are an example of a kind of 'typical interview' talk that allows the recognised roles of IR and IE to come into being in a way that creates the context necessary for a particular kind of institutional relationship: in this case, the interview that we see in Extract 5. Similarly, ten Have's (1991) work on doctor-patient interaction demonstrates how the asymmetrical relationship created by the use of 'typical' doctor/patient talk acts not only as a constraint on interaction but also as a resource. In positioning each other as 'doctor' and 'patient', the interactants create a framework that provides structure and strategies for successful interaction. The benefits of asking extended and repeated questions are that they provide a handy and effective framework by which the conversation may proceed.

However, the benefits of this framework are not always equally shared between IR and IE. In Extract 5, we see how the repetition of the IR's question becomes potentially problematic as the IR appears to struggle to elicit any additional information from the IE. The effect of the IR mentioning a prior topic (line 5) in this case could be understood by the IE as implying that their earlier contribution is not considered a sufficient answer and either an elaboration or another answer is needed. So, with our recommendations for interviewers in mind, it is important to notice that if an IR gets a response from the participant that is not 'sufficient', and they want to try to elicit more, the IR should always allow for the possibility that there might not be anything else that the interviewee wants to add.

Recommendation
A recommendation based on the above extract could be for interviewers to consider asking the interviewee more explicitly whether they want to add more by saying something like 'is there something else you want to say about this topic?' or 'would you like to add something else?' and accepting that there is the possibility of no further response.

Conclusion

The conversation analysis presented in this chapter highlighted the collaborative notion of interviews that is required in order to achieve intersubjective understanding and to generate data for thematic analysis. As Roulston (2014) suggests, examining *how* speakers manage interactional problems can help researchers identify trouble sources and important issues for further investigations. The five extracts from the data presented above illustrate a number of features of interviewers' talk that play an important role in constructing the interviewees' responses. The following contributions were made by the interviewers which were problematised by interviewees: offering candidate words such as *rarity*, abandoning the question, closing topics by producing formulations which are hard to disagree with, repetition to elicit answers and restating previously mentioned topics. What is also interesting to note is how those different contributions from the interviewer interact within the same extract and happen in different combinations (such as in Extract 1 and Extract 3). Furthermore, Roulston (2014) suggests that in instances when interviewees decline to provide elaborate answers, such as in Extract 5 in our data, instead of rejecting such answers as uninformative responses, interviewers and researcher can use that data to improve their understanding of the ways in which interview participants co-construct their versions of the world into being.

In line with our analysis of the contributions made by the interviewers in our data, we have developed a list of recommendations for researchers and/or community activists to consider when preparing for interviews.

Recommendation 1: if an interviewer notices that they have made a specific contribution, such as offering a word that narrowed the range of choices that the interviewee was presented with, they can consider following it up with a more general contribution such as 'is there something else you want to say?' or 'do you have some more comments about this topic?'.

Recommendation 2: if an interviewer notices that an interviewee problematises their question, an interviewer can consider replying with 'yes' or 'anything' followed by a pause. This way an interviewer can avoid adding more information to the original question and only confirm that the interviewee has understood the question as was intended.

Recommendation 3: if an interviewer notices that their contribution was judgemental or changed the direction of the answer, they can repeat the original question. This, of course, could result in the interviewee repeating their answer or changing it. However, this technique may provide an opportunity for the interviewee to clarify their answer. An additional suggestion here could be for an interviewer to consider asking the interviewee to summarise their answer.

Recommendation 4: if an interviewer notices that the interviewee has not responded within five seconds of the question, let the silence be. Longer pauses allow time for the interviewee to think of answers. This can potentially lead to more detailed and interesting answers.

Recommendation 5: if an interviewer feels an answer from the interviewee is insufficient, consider asking them if they want to add more by saying 'is there something else you want to say about this topic?' and accept the possibility of no further response.

An additional recommendation for anyone planning to conduct interviews is to present the interviewee with some ground rules at the beginning of an interview. For example, a ground rule about silence could be established by the interviewer by saying 'I am going to ask you questions and I will leave some time for you to think, so there may be silence. If you do not understand my question, please ask'. This ground rule may help to normalise silence and the possibility of miscommunication. Furthermore, it will allow for the fact that it is acceptable for the interviewee to ask questions, giving them more power in the interview context.

As was illustrated in the analysis, some interviewers' contributions may have a constraining effect on interviewee's response, and interviewers are advised to be aware of the potential for this to happen. However, it is important to stress that by proposing the recommendations above we are not suggesting that any more authentic or true stories can be elicited but that, in taking account of the recommendations, a wide range of answers may be achieved. All answers will always be situated and co-constructed— but we suggest that in giving interviewees more time to understand their questions and come up with detailed answers, it is not truth that results, but rather *interesting, detailed stories.* Given that the York's Hidden Stories project aimed to find out and share stories from/for York's hidden community, the more detail in the stories, the more successful the project.

It is also important for interviewers to give careful consideration to constructing questions when preparing for an interview. In line with constructionist ideas about interviews, mentioned in Chap. 1, questions can never be neutral, but a careful consideration when it comes to formulating questions can help both an interviewer and interviewees to have a better understanding of the data produced at an interview as well as the data analysis. Pomerantz and Zemel (2003) discuss two ways in which interviewer's questions express their perspectives when it comes to interviewing. They examine two way of packaging questions: This is a publicly known problem; What is your solution? and This is a matter of public debate; What is your position? It is suggested that the former formulation presents interviewee with an issue as a problem which implicates an assumption that interviewee agrees, whereas the latter formulation implies that the issues are a matter of debate, which indicates that there are or may be multiple views of the subject. This is a useful suggestion which can be considered when designing questions for an interview.

It is important for interviewers to know that conversational difficulties can occur during an interview. Pomerantz and Zemel (2003: 229) describe two types of conversational difficulties that were observed in their data: (1) 'the interviewee's perspective differs from the perspective implied by the query, and (2) the interviewee's basis for a position is other than what he or she thinks the interviewer will take it to be'. Interviewees and interviewers can make adjustments when such interactional difficulties happen, for example, interviewers can ask follow-up questions to allow the interviewee to confirm their understanding or offer a different perspective. It is important to emphasise that the process of noticing conversational difficulties requires practice and self-reflection; this can be developed by listening back to the recordings of previous interviews.

It could be argued that meaning is always co-constructed and this cannot be avoided. However, by paying attention to the suggested recommendations, it is possible that interviewers may be able to become more sensitive to the interactional consequences of their contributions. Furthermore, it may also be possible to raise interviewees' awareness about how their stories get co-constructed with their audiences, meaning that an outcome of a storytelling project could be to raise the participants' awareness that their stories are not theirs alone, but are co-constructed every time they are retold to a different audience. If this were the case, the recommendations offered above could be useful to help interviewees exercise more control over the construction of their own stories.

References

Ameka, F. (1992). Interjections: The universal yet neglected part of speech. *Journal of Pragmatics, 18*(2–3), 101–118.

Bolden, G. B. (2009). Implementing incipient actions: The discourse marker 'so' in English conversation. *Journal of Pragmatics, 41*(5), 974–998.

Cotton, K. (1988). *Classroom questioning.* Northwest Regional Educational Laboratory.

Coulmas, F. (Ed.). (1986). *Direct and indirect speech.* Berlin: Mouton de Gruyter'.

Craig, G., Adamson, S., Ali, N., & Demsash, F. (2010). *Mapping rapidly changing minority ethnic populations: A case study of York.* Joseph Rowntree Foundation. [Online]. Retrieved March 20, 2019, from www.jrf.org.uk/publications/changing-minority-ethnic-populations.

Cruz, M. P. (2009). Towards an alternative relevance-theoretic approach to inter-jections. *International Review of Pragmatics*, 1(1), 182–206.

Edmondson, W., & House, J. (1991). Do learners talk too much? The waffle phe-nomenon in interlanguage pragmatics. In R. Phillipson, E. Kellerman, L. Selinker, M. Sharwood-Smith, & M. Swain (Eds.), *Foreign/second language pedagogy research*. Clevedon: Multilingual Matters.

Fox Tree, J. E., & Schrock, J. C. (2002). Basic meanings of you know and I mean. *Journal of Pragmatics*, 34(6), 727–747.

Gardner, R. (2001). *When listeners talk: Response tokens and listener stance*. Amsterdam; Philadelphia: John Benjamins Publishing Company.

Gardner, R. (2004). On delaying the answer: Question sequences extended after the question. In R. Gardner & J. Wagner (Eds.), *Second language conversations*. London: Continuum.

Hak, T. (2003). Interviewer laughter as an unspecified request for clarification. In H. van de Berg, M. Wergerell, & H. Houtkoop-Steenstara (Eds.), *Analysing race talk: Multidisciplinary approaches to the interview*. Cambridge: Cambridge University Press.

ten Have, P. (1991). Talk and institution: A reconsideration of the 'asymmetry' of doctor-patient interaction. In D. Boden & D. H. Zimmerman (Eds.), *Talk and social structure: Studies in ethnomethodology and conversation analysis*. Cambridge: Polity Press.

Heritage, J. (1984). A change-of-state-token end aspects of its sequential place-ment. In J. M. Atkinson & J. Heritage (Eds.), *Structures of social action: Studies in conversation analysis* (pp. 299–345). Cambridge, UK: Cambridge University Press.

Heritage, J., & Robinson, J. D. (2011). Some versus any medical issues: Encouraging patients to reveal their unmet concerns. In C. Antaki (Ed.), *Applied conversation analysis: Intervention and change in institutional talk*. Basingstoke: Palgrave.

Heritage, J. C., & Watson, D. R. (1979). Formulations as conversational objects. In G. Psathas (Ed.), *Everyday language: Studies in ethnomethodology*. New York: Irvington.

Holt, E. (1996). Reporting on talk: The use of direct reported speech in conversa-tion. *Research on Language and Social Interaction*, 29(3), 219–245.

Holt, E. (2017). Indirect reported speech in storytelling: Its position, design, and uses. *Research on Language and Social Interaction*, 50(2), 171–187.

Jefferson, G., Sacks, H., & Schegloff, E. A. (1987). Notes on laugher in the pur-suit of intimacy. In G. Button & J. R. E. Lee (Eds.), *Talk and social organisa-tion* (pp. 152–205). Clevedon: Multilingual Matters.

Lee, D. A. (2003). Constructivist processes in discourse: A cognitive linguistics perspective. In H. van den Berg, M. Wetherell, & H. Houtkoop-Steenstra (Eds.), *Analyzing race talk*. Cambridge: Cambridge University Press.

Mann, S. (2016). *The research interview: Reflective practice and reflexivity in research processes.* Basingstoke: Palgrave Macmillan.

The Office for National Statistics (2014). Migration Statistics Quarterly Report, August 2014 [Online] Available at: www.ons.gov.uk/ons/rel/migration1/migration-statistics-quarterly-report/august-2014/stb-msqr-august-2014.html.

Peters, P., & Wong, D. (2015). Turn management and backchannels. In K. Aijmer & C. Rühlemann (Eds.), *Corpus pragmatics: A handbook* (pp. 408–429). Cambridge: Cambridge University Press.

Pomerantz, A. (1986). Extreme case formulations: A way of legitimizing claims. *Human Studies, 9*(2/3), 219–229.

Pomerantz, A., & Zemel, A. (2003). Perspectives and frameworks in interviewers' queries. In H. van de Berg, M. Wertherell, & H. Houtkoop-Steenstara (Eds.), *Analysing race talk: Multidisciplinary approaches to the interview.* Cambridge: Cambridge University Press.

Puchta, C., & Potter, J. (1999). Asking elaborate questions: Focus groups and the management of spontaneity. *Journal of Sociolinguistics, 3,* 314–335.

Rapley, T. J. (2001). The art(fulness) of open-ended interviewing: Some considerations on analysing interviews. *Qualitative Research, 1*(3), 303–323.

Roulston, K. (2014). Interactional problems in research interviews. *Qualitative Research, 14*(3), 227–293.

Rowe, M. B. (1987). Wait-time: Slowing down may be a way of speeding up. *American Educator, 11*(47), 38–43.

Schegloff, E. A. (1982). Discourse as an interactional achievement: Some uses of 'uh huh' and other things that come between sentences. In D. Tannen (Ed.), *Analyzing discourse: Text and talk* (pp. 71–93). Washington, DC: Georgetown University Press.

Stahl, R. J. (1994). Using 'think-time' and 'wait-time' skillfully in the classroom. *ERIC Digest, 6.*

Tama, M. C. (1989). Critical thinking: Promoting it in the classroom. *ERIC Digest, 6.*

Wicaksono, R. (2012). 'Raising students' awareness of the construction of communicative (in)competence in international classrooms. In J. Ryan (Ed.), *Cross cultural teaching and learning for home and international students: Internationalisation of pedagogy and curriculum in higher education.* London; New York: Routledge.

Wierzbicka, A. (1992). The semantics of interjection. *Journal of Pragmatics, 18*(2–3), 159–192.

Wilkins, D. P. (1992). Interjections as deictics. *Journal of Pragmatics, 18*(2–3), 119–158.

CHAPTER 5

Conclusions

Abstract This chapter draws conclusions and discusses the limitations of the case study presented in our book. A set of recommendations is outlined here for the use of interviews as part of community projects where the discovery of hidden stories is an aim. The case study is an example of a research project from conception to completion, telling the stories of the participants and critically reflecting on how knowledge is (re)created in an interview context.

Keywords Conclusion • Limitations • Recommendations • Reflections

Finally, in this chapter, we draw some conclusions from our case study and summarise the recommendations based on our analysis of the data. The middle section of this chapter discusses the limitations of our two chosen methods as well as ways in which two different analytical perspectives can co-exist and complement each other in one research study. At the end of the chapter, we reflect on the partnership between us, applied linguists, and our client, the Centre for Global Education York.

In summary, the case study we describe in this book was designed to answer the following two research questions.

© The Author(s) 2020
R. Wicaksono, D. Zhurauskaya, *York's Hidden Stories,*
https://doi.org/10.1057/978-1-137-55839-8_5

Research question one: What themes occur in the interviews with York's Black, Asian and Minority Ethnic residents on the topics identified by our client (i.e. reasons, values and barriers)?

Thematic analysis was used to answer the above question. The analysis showed that the main reasons for immigrating to the UK, presented by the participants in the interviews conducted by the community project workers, were to study, work or join family. A small number of participants had arrived in York as children, accompanying parents who came to York for work, or as refugees. The participants' account of their values used words such as respect, family, friends, loyalty, honesty, generosity, difference, education, faith and community. When asked about barriers in their lives, the participants mentioned being accepted by their spouse's family, being mixed race in the 80s, difference, lack of confidence, gender discrimination in the workplace, poverty, divorce, prejudice in their own community, getting an education, missing 'home', racism, settling down, language, limitations on travel, and perfectionism.

Research question two: How do the interviewers' contributions shape the interaction with the interviewees?

Using conversation analysis to analyse the interview data demonstrated how the interviewers' contributions had an interactional effect on the interviewees' talk. Examples included offering words as examples of possible answers, abandoning questions, closing topics by producing formulations that are hard to disagree with, repetition to elicit answers and restating previously mentioned topics.

The two analyses presented in our study provide an example of how one might critically examine the same dataset, depending on the aims of the research and the researchers'/clients' beliefs about the nature of communication and the construction of meaning. Two possible readings of our interview data were presented in Chap. 4 of this book:

1. a report of the themes mentioned by the project participants during the interviews, as in the thematic analysis;
2. a display of interactional contributions made by the interview participants, as in the conversation analysis.

Indeed, there are always a number of ways in which a researcher can look at their data. As researchers, the choices we make depend on a variety of factors, including what we want to find out (the aims of the research) and our beliefs about, for example, knowledge, meaning and communication. We hope that this book has demonstrated how interview data can be understood and used in several different ways, including to provide insight into:

- another person's experience (a belief we described as neo-positivist);
- another person's *real* (hidden) experience (a belief we described as romantic);
- how people tell their stories in ways that meet their immediate, or longer term, needs in specific situations (constructionist);
- how accepted roles and the responsibilities associated with them (such as the 'interviewer' being in control with an expectation to ask questions, change topics and decide when the interview is finished) constrain how people behave and what they say and how these constraints may, to a certain extent, be resisted and thereby changed (transformative).

Two possible readings of our interview data are as a basis for:

- a report of the themes mentioned by the project participants during the interviews, as in the thematic analysis (a neo-positivist/romantic approach);
- a display of interactional contributions made by the interview participants, as in the conversation analysis (a constructionist approach with some elements of a transformative approach).

RECOMMENDATIONS

An outcome of the conversation analysis that was conducted to address research question two was a set of recommendations for community workers who want to use interviews as part of their projects. It is important to acknowledge that these are recommendations for possible noticings that are based on our analysis of the data, collected in one context, and are not, therefore, presented as prescriptions for the management of all interviews. Instead, they are representative of a type of sensitivity (to the interactional effects of questions, answers and responses to answers) that interviewers can aim to develop, sensitivity that is deployed both 'online', as the interview is taking place, and 'offline' when the interviewer analyses/uses their data.

Recommendation 1: if an interviewer notices that they have made a specific contribution, such as offering a word that narrowed the range of choices that the interviewee was presented with, they can consider following it up with a more general contribution such as 'is there something else you want to say?' or 'do you have some more comments about this topic?'.

Recommendation 2: if an interviewer notices that an interviewee problematises their question, an interviewer can consider replying with 'yes' or 'anything' followed by a pause. This way an interviewer can avoid adding more information to the original question and focus on confirming that the interviewee has satisfied themselves that they have an understanding of the question.

Recommendation 3: if an interviewer notices that their response to an interviewee's answer was overtly judgemental or seemed to change the direction of the answer, they can try repeating the original question. This, of course, could result in the interviewee repeating their answer or changing it. However, this technique may provide an opportunity for the interviewee to add to their answer. An additional suggestion here could be for an interviewer to consider asking the interviewee to summarise their answer.

Recommendation 4: if an interviewer notices that the interviewee has not responded within five seconds of the question, let the silence be. Longer pauses allow time for the interviewee to think of answers. This can potentially lead to more detailed and interesting answers.

Recommendation 5: if an interviewer feels an answer from the interviewee is insufficient, consider asking them if they want to add more by saying 'is there something else you want to say about this topic?' and accept that there is the possibility of no further response.

Having made these recommendations, however, we cannot be sure that telling them to an interviewer will make any difference to the way in which they conduct an interview. Much more research is needed into the role of training/experience in increasing sensitivity to the interactional consequences of questioning and on the degree to which this sensitivity is useful while questioning. Having said this, Richards (2011: 99) appears optimistic, suggesting that applied conversation analysis (and 'other' approaches to interview analysis) can be used, 'for the purposes of data analysis or improving technique, or both' and that in 'developing sensitivity to aspects of one's talk makes it more likely that shifts of this sort [in, for example, the type of minimal responses used] will be noticed'. As Richards says, there is no 'case for more detailed prescriptions regarding interview behaviour, but rather the opposite: a reminder that progress depends on the development of craft skills through the sensitive interrogation of one's own work' (2011: 107). It is very important to acknowledge that the recommendations suggested here are not prescriptions for all interviews but suggestions for how they might be managed. As Richards says, it is through careful reflection on our own interviewing skills that researchers can try to develop their craft, a process of development that is self-generated, not instructed, and which is acutely aware of the benefits and limitations of our choices.

LIMITATIONS

In the next section of this chapter, we explore the advantages and disadvantages of our two methods: thematic analysis and conversation analysis.

Thematic Analysis

Thematic analysis of spoken data has both advantages and disadvantages. An advantage of thematic analysis is 'the sensitivity to recurrent motifs salient in participants' stories' and, therefore, the ability to highlight what is important to interviewees that may not have been reflected previously (Pavlenko 2007: 166). Kitzinger (2011) outlines two further advantages of thematic analysis, both of which were apparent in this study. Firstly, thematic analysis is useful to systematise information and feedback for the researcher/organisation that is collecting the data. Secondly, this type of analysis can be used to summarise key recurrent themes in the data in a way that might be useful for the researcher/organisation to report back to their funders. More specifically, on that point, the results of the thematic analysis 'take a form that is readily accessible to the educated general public, and results can be relatively quickly produced' (Kitzinger 2011: 100). In the case of this study, the advantages of the thematic analysis were twofold. Firstly, the results of the thematic analysis were able to help the client to gain some (new) understanding of participants' experiences (accessibility). Secondly, the thematic analysis provided a (systematic) resource which represented the full range of participants' reasons for migration, values and barriers. This was an advantage both for the client and, as a preliminary analytical step, for us as applied linguists, interested as we are in the ways in which interlocutors use language and what effects different linguistic features have on the interaction.

On the other hand, the disadvantage of thematic analysis is that it can be seen as a simplistic approach to understanding what people say, its findings representing only a very superficial representation of the reality of participants' experiences. The rationale for the thematic categories, the relationship between the categories and the matching of the examples to the categories are not always made clear by the researcher. Where there is a justification for the thematic categories, this is often on the basis of perceived repetition in the data, meaning that potentially important topics, which are less frequently mentioned or (perhaps because they are so 'obvious' or taboo) not mentioned at all, are lost in the analysis (Talmy 2010).

Furthermore, the results of a thematic analysis are in danger of being very closely aligned to the pre-existing beliefs of the interviewer, given the difficulty of avoiding the tendency to see what we expect to see. And finally, the pressure on interviewees to conform to what they think the expectations of the interviewer are may mean that the themes that emerge from the analysis do not represent the beliefs/experiences of the interviewee, but those they judge to be acceptable to the interviewer. Neopositivist and romantic beliefs about the value of interview data may be seriously undermined by these disadvantages of thematic analysis.

Conversation Analysis

Perhaps the main advantage of conversation analysis is that it allows for a fine-grained observation of the data, which makes it possible to identify features of talk that otherwise might be overlooked. Analysts aim to show the intricate ways in which speakers and listeners mutually organise their talk and what these ways tell us about socially preferred patterns of interaction, including turn-taking, opening and closing an interaction, introducing and changing topics, managing misunderstanding, introducing bad news, agreeing and disagreeing, eliciting a response by asking a question and so on. Conversation analysts argue that this focus on the conversational activities found in an extract of talk is the only justifiable analytical focus and researchers should avoid imposing their own assumptions, including what they believe to be 'contextual factors' on the data (Schegloff 1991). Drew and Heritage (1992), however, remind us that interviews are institutionally framed, meaning that they happen at a pre-arranged time and place, and often have a hidden, pre-organised agenda in mind that is dictated by the interviewers. During the interview, phrases such as 'the first question I'm going to ask you' and 'now let's move on to the next question', set the dynamics of the interviewer-interviewee relationship, giving the interviewers more power in the interview context and making it essential, they argue, for interviewers to be aware of the contributions they make to the interview data, and for those contributions to be inspected as part of the formal data analysis.

Some possible drawbacks of conversation analysts' focus on the delicate machinery of interaction have been highlighted by, for example, critical linguists (see Wetherell 1998). Critics of conversation analysis have said that the sole focus on the conversational activities found in extracts of talk blinds analysts to the ideological aspects of language and to text production as social practice. Debates between conversation analytic- and critically-oriented analysts inevitably focus on the different emphases of their approach (see, in particular, the exchanges between Billig (1999a, b) and Schegloff (1999a, b)). But these differences should not be overplayed; Billig reminds us that he

> share[s] Schegloff's unease about studies which pronounce on the nature of discourses, without getting down to the business of studying what is actually uttered or written. (Billig 1999a: 544)

In this study, our client's requirement for a thematic analysis of the data meant that our knowledge of the context provided a useful and interesting backdrop to the conversation analysis. This is not to say that either the thematic analysis or the conversation analysis could not have stood alone—they both could; the former would have satisfied our client and the latter might have interested other linguists/conversation analysts. But the backdrop provided by the thematic analysis paved the way (for our client) to a less familiar way of analysing data and may have helped to demonstrate to them why our answers to research question one are, necessarily, very provisional. Furthermore, given that the themes were identified in advance by our client, the selection of extracts from our data for transcription was easier to justify to a non-specialist audience, potentially increasing the interest in, and uptake of, the recommendations generated by our conversation analysis.

As far as the reporting of our study in this book, we have attempted to pay attention to a framework first developed by Potter and Hepburn (2012) for adding credibility to interview research (see also Silverman 2017), aiming to:

- improve the transparency of the interview set-up in which our data was collected
- attend fully to the actions of the interviewers
- connect our analytic observations to specific elements of the interviews
- improve analysis of our data by showing how the interviews (and the analysis of the interview data) are permeated by the interviewers', and our own, assumptions about interviews and their participants, as well as the interviewer's project-based needs (to satisfy, e.g. funders and our own research agendas)
- show how interviewees respond to the various activities and categories offered by the interviewer
- show how the interviewers can make some responses to their questions seem relevant or interesting or remain silent and have the opposite effect
- avoid assuming that people communicate in ways that are related to 'who they really are' but recognise that how our behaviour is perceived depends on who is perceiving (and where and when).

Bringing Neo-positivist/Romantic, Constructionist and Transformative Perspectives Together

The 'two different cultures' of interviews as research instruments for finding out what participants think/know, and interviews as research topics/co-constructions (Van den Berg et al. 2003: 5), are not necessarily as far apart as they may seem, or, indeed, as we may have presented them in Chap. 1 of this book. At least in applied linguistics, both thematic analysis and conversation analysis may, depending on the aims of the research project, have a useful part to play, depending on the needs of our client and the importance of a pragmatic approach to meeting these needs. We would not want to use 'pragmatism' as a reason for not thinking very carefully about our choices, however. Indeed, we hope that in this book we were able to demonstrate the importance of paying attention to the theories of interviewing when conducting qualitative applied linguistics studies, as suggested by Talmy (2010: 143):

> there is considerable need for heightened reflexivity about the interview methods that applied linguistics researchers use in their studies, on the role of the interviewer in occasioning interview answers, on the subject 'behind'

the interviewee, on the status ascribed to interview data, and on how those data are analyzed and represented, regardless of whether one opts to conceive of interviews as research instrument, or research interviews as participation in social practices.

Given that the work of applied linguists is based on solving real-world, language-related problems, it seems likely that we will come across a variety of perspectives on language and communication, as well as on 'reality', knowledge and society. These perspectives will, inevitably, result in a range of different ideas about how to do research, what the research findings mean and how they can/should be used. As the case study reported here shows, our client approached the aims and uses of the interviews from a 'romantic' perspective, whereas as applied linguistics, we were more closely aligned with constructionist ideas about interview data. Based on our experiences during this study, we tentatively suggest that applied linguists engage in an open dialogue with clients, with caution, but without abandoning their own theoretical beliefs. Our position may differ from the experience of other researchers. Mazeland and ten Have (1996), for example, describe how they had to, reluctantly, leave their 'comfortable' position of what they describe as 'ethnomethodological indifference', in order to engage in debate with interviewers who were not linguists. Perhaps this is a difference between applied linguists and researchers in other disciplines, including linguistics. Given that the applied linguist's job is to focus on recognising real-world problems in which there are language-related issues and/or to respond to the identification of a problem by a potential client (Hall et al. 2017), we are used to the idea of collaboration and negotiation with different perspectives and do not see these processes as obstructive of our research, but as an essential and interesting part of it.

The nature and scope of the problem we explored during this study turned out to be somewhat different than the problem that was initially identified by our client, the Centre for Global Education York. Some of the answers/solutions we offered to the client were to the problem that they had identified, and others were solutions to a problem that they had not realised existed (Atkinson and Silverman 1997). This was a very sensitive issue, and careful communication with the client, rather than compromise, was needed. Taking our client's worlds seriously, not as versions of a world, but as different worlds that exist in parallel with our own, is something we have tried to achieve in this study. Recognition of different 'realities' is a relatively new challenge in applied linguistics, but one which we very much need to face. Different ontological commitments can have a very important impact on the beliefs and behaviour, not only of researchers but of the participants in our research and the clients we serve (Hall and Wicaksono 2020). Failure to acknowledge and explore our different conceptualisations can result in misunderstanding, even conflict, and ineffective or inappropriate recommendations or policy advice. On the other hand, working with our clients to understand the ontological assumptions that underpin each other's ideologies can help us to negotiate, for example, project aims and desired outcomes. Furthermore, trying to understand what we and others recognise as, for example, 'interview', 'value', 'treasure', 'theme', 'summary' and so on can help to avoid assuming that we agree on what these things are and what counts as an example of them. Finally, critical examination of our ontologies of ideas such a 'local' and 'home' (which may be so familiar to us that we have forgotten that they are 'only' ideas) could help in efforts by applied linguists to expose and contest the social injustices faced by many migrants to York and around the world (Wicaksono and Hall 2020).

The testing and evaluation of the solutions we proposed in the recommendations section of this study is, of course, the responsibility of the clients, who are the ones with access to the site of the problem initially identified. At this stage in the research, it is our client's decision whether to continue to involve us, given that participation in solution-testing was not initially agreed. We are currently working on negotiating the next steps in our project with them.

Our Final Reflections

In the final section of our book, we ask ourselves a question 'so what?'. It is a question that provides an end to our study, a chance to summarise what we have learned and reflect on the significance of this learning. It also helps us to think about what we might have done differently and what we could do next.

We have learned that interviews look so familiar that they have almost become invisible as a cultural construct. Their framing and constraining effects, on relationships and identities/personal histories, are so familiar to us as to be unremarkable. It is the job of applied linguists to point out that interviews are an opportunity for a story to be projected or constrained/rejected, a site of creative struggle, of innovation and destruction. We should demonstrate the delicate mechanisms through which this struggle takes place, including the effects of repetition, silence, overlap and the many other features we described in Chap. 4 of this book.

In accordance with Rapley (2019), we have attempted to show that when using interviews as research instruments, equal attention and analytic consideration needs to be applied to

> pre- and post- interview talk, to moments of sampling, recruitment and consent, to the preparation of and adjustments to interview guides, and most importantly, to recover the different times, spaces and places, of the 'desk work' for doing analysis on interviews. (Rapley 2019: 282)

We have learned that the clients of applied linguists, and the participants on our research, may have very different ideas about the aims of research and the meaning/use of data. These differences are interesting, and need to form part of the research process as we work out what we all mean by familiar concepts/acts such as 'question', 'home', 'value' and so on. Not taking the time to work out how we conceptualise these aspects of 'common sense' is a missed opportunity for collaboration and depletes the value of the research findings.

We have learned that it is possible to do research on interviews that treat the interaction both as content (a neo-positivist or romantic conceptualisation of the interview) and discourse (a constructionist or transformative approach). And that these approaches do conflict with each other conceptually but, very importantly, that this conflict can provide a good way into an ontologically-aware type of public engagement that is typical of applied linguistics.

We have learned that people are not just 'themselves' (a neo-positivist/romantic assumption), and don't only exist in relation to each other (a constructionist assumption), but that they also 'intra-act' (Barad 2007) with material things, including inorganic objects (such as a recording device, a car), technologies (such as a transcription code, music) and non-human organisms (such as pets and plants).

We have learned that what seemed like binary categories, one versus another, interviewer versus interviewee, content versus discourse, academic versus public, are actually fluid, dynamic concepts that are continually emerging in interaction as a result of what people think 'is', what they think they know, and what they believe is fair (see Toohey 2019). Instead of defending our territory (be that a place, a familiar generalisation, a research method or an institution), we could open up ourselves, and our clients and research participants, to the infinite undoing of endings/conclusions and therefore the possibility of new histories. We could acknowledge the transformative power of 'just' observing. And we could point to our interconnectedness and therefore the importance of our obligations to each other.

We have also discovered that York has 'hidden' diversity, in a variety of respects, and that improving awareness of difference is probably a way of becoming comfortable with difference, rather than feeling threatened by it, or threatened by other peoples' fear of it. On the other hand, the opportunity to tell our 'own' story is often welcomed, and the aspects of our story that we may like to stress are those that we think differ from other stories. There is always a tension between wanting to be 'ourselves' and wanting to be part of something else. Storytelling is one way of constantly negotiating that tension, against the constantly changing backdrop of the city, as it exists in 'reality' and in our minds.

What we could have done differently and what we could do next are the same thing. We could have built in an evaluation phase in to the research. On the other hand, when we set off on this project, we didn't anticipate that a series of recommendations for community project interviews would be an outcome of our research. It was probably an error of planning not to assume that something would come out of our study that would need testing with the help of our client. So, next, we would like to design a new study that looks at the effectiveness of awareness-raising activities for interviewers, and which also works with 'hidden' individuals and groups to collaborate on ways of them telling their stories.

FINAL NOTE (OF CAUTION)

We are writing the last chapter of this book during the isolating experience of 'lockdown', when the opportunity to tell our stories is limited by the need to stay at home. New ways of creating our identities online are already available, and we look forward to exploring how these, in addition to the more familiar face-to-face activities, can be used to unhide the worlds of those who may previously have been hidden.

However, we are also writing against a backdrop of political unrest in Belarus, where there is a popular protest against the President, who has been in power since 1994. These protests began with a blogger, Syarhei Tsikhanouski, who started travelling around Belarus, collecting stories from people that were unheard of on state TV. Tsikhanouski and other opposition candidates have gained strong support from the people who were watching their stories on the internet. However, those stories were unpopular with the current government, who in due course jailed the blogger, his team and other opposition candidates. Throughout this book, we have focused on the positive aspects of storytelling and how telling stories can help to 'unhide' 'hidden' (aspects of) peoples' lives. However, as the example of the Belarusian blogger shows, stories can also be suppressed and storytellers silenced. Unfortunately, some people are prepared to go a long way to stop other people from telling their stories. Fortunately, there are other people who are prepared to go an even longer way to continue telling their stories. We are listening.

References

Atkinson, P., & Silverman, D. (1997). Kundera's immortality: The interview society and the invention of the self. *Qualitative Inquiry, 3*(3), 304–325.

Barad, K. (2007). *Meeting the universe halfway: Quantum physics and the entanglement of matter and meaning.* Durham: Duke University Press.

Billig, M. (1999a). Whose terms? Whose ordinariness? Rhetoric and ideology in Conversation Analysis. *Discourse and Society, 10*(4), 543–558.

Billig, M. (1999b). Conversation Analysis and the claims of naivety. *Discourse and Society, 10*(4), 572–576.

Drew, P. and Heritage, J. (Eds.) (1992). *Talk at work: Interaction in institutional settings.* Cambridge: Cambridge University Press.

Hall, C. J., & Wicaksono, R. (2020). Approaching ontologies of English. In C. J. Hall & R. Wicaksono (Eds.), *Ontologies of English: Conceptualising the language for learning, teaching, and assessment* (pp. 3–12). Cambridge: Cambridge University Press.

Hall, C. J., Smith, P. H., & Wicaksono, R. (2017). *Mapping applied linguistics: An introduction for students and practitioners.* Abingdon: Routledge.

Kitzinger, C. (2011). Working with childbirth helplines: The contributions and limitations of conversation analysis. In C. Antaki (Ed.), *Applied conversation analysis: Intervention and change in institutional talk* (pp. 98–118). Basingstoke: Palgrave Macmillan.

Mazeland, H., & ten Have, P. (1996). Essential tensions in (semi-) open research interviews. In I. Maso & D. Wester (Eds.), *The deliberate dialogue: Qualitative perspectives on the interview.* Brussels: VUB University Press.

Pavlenko, A. (2007). Autobiographic narratives as data in applied linguistics. *Applied Linguistics, 28*(2), 163–188.

Potter, J., & Hepburn, A. (2012). Eight challenges for interview researchers. In J. F. Gubrium, J. A. Holstein, A. Marvasti, & K. McKinney (Eds.), *The Sage handbook of interview research: The complexity of the craft* (pp. 555–570). Los Angeles: Sage.

Rapley, T. (2019). The way(s) of interviewing. Exploring social studies of interviews. In K. Roulston (Ed.), *Interactional studies of qualitative research interviews* (pp. 271–282). Amsterdam; Philadelphia: John Benjamins Publishing Company.

Richards, K. (2011). Using micro-analysis in interviewer training: 'Continuers' and interviewer positioning. *Applied Linguistics, 32*(1), 95–112.

Schegloff, E. A. (1991). Reflecting on talk and social structure. In D. Boden & D. Zimmerman (Eds.), *Talk and social structure*. Cambridge: Polity.

Schegloff, E. A. (1999a). Schegloff's texts' as Billig's data: A critical reply. *Discourse and Society, 10*(4), 558–572.

Schegloff, E. A. (1999b). Naivete vs sophistication or discipline vs self-indulgence: A rejoinder to Billig. *Discourse and Society, 10*(4), 577–582.

Silverman, D. (2017). How was it for you? The Interview Society and the irresistible rise of the (poorly analyzed) interview. *Qualitative Research, 17*(2), 144–158.

Talmy, S. (2010). Qualitative interviews in applied linguistics: From research instrument to social practice. *Annual Review of Applied Linguistics, 30*, 128–148.

The Office for National Statistics (2014). Migration Statistics Quarterly Report, August 2014 [Online] Available at: www.ons.gov.uk/ons/rel/migration1/migration-statistics-quarterly-report/august-2014/stb-msqr-august-2014.html.

Toohey, K. (2019). The onto-epistemologies of New Materialism: Implications for applied linguistics pedagogies and research. *Applied Linguistics, 40*(6), 937–956.

Van den Berg, H., Wetherell, M., & Houtkoop-Steenstra, H. (Eds.). (2003). *Analyzing race talk: Multidisciplinary approaches to the interview*. Cambridge: Cambridge University Press.

Wetherell, M. (1998). Positioning and interpretive repertoires: Conversation analysis and post-structuralism in dialogue. *Discourse and Society, 9*(3), 387–412.

Wicaksono, R., & Hall, C. J. (2020). Using ontologies of English'. In C. J. Hall & R. Wicaksono (Eds.), *Ontologies of English: Conceptualising the language for learning, teaching, and assessment* (pp. 368–376). Cambridge: Cambridge University Press.

APPENDIX

Jefferson	transcription	system	(Jefferson	2004)
A: word word [word] B: [word]	Overlapping speech			
word	Emphasis			
WORD	Louder than surrounding speech			
°word°	Quieter speech			
(0.4)	Timed pauses			
(.)	A micropause, too short to measure			
((laughter))	Additional comments from the transcriber, e.g. about features of context or delivery			
wo::rd	Elongation of the prior sound; the more colons, the more elongation			
hh	Out-breaths			
.hh	In-breaths			
↑word	Higher pitch: denotes a higher shift in pitch			
↓word	Lower pitch: denotes a lower shift in pitch			
wor-	A cut-off of the preceding sound			
>word<	Speeded-up talk			
<word>	Slower talk			
word= =word	Immediate 'latching' of successive talk, whether of one or more speakers, with no interval			
heh heh	Voiced laughter			

© The Author(s) 2020
R. Wicaksono, D. Zhurauskaya, *York's Hidden Stories*,
https://doi.org/10.1057/978-1-137-55839-8

REFERENCES

Ameka, F. (1992). Interjections: The universal yet neglected part of speech. *Journal of Pragmatics, 18*(2–3), 101–118.

Antaki, C. (2011a). Six kinds of applied conversation analysis. In C. Antaki (Ed.), *Applied conversation analysis: Intervention and change in institutional talk.* Houndmills, Basingstoke: Palgrave Macmillan.

Antaki, C. (2011b). Ten guidelines for changing names in transcripts. *An Introduction to Conversation Analysis.* [Online]. Retrieved September 20, 2019, from http://ca-tutorials.lboro.ac.uk/pseudos2.htm.

Antaki, C., Billig, M., Edwards, D., & Potter, J. (2003). Discourse analysis means doing analysis: A critique of six analytic shortcomings. *Discourse Analysis Online, 1*(1). [Online]. Retrieved September 20, 2015, from https://extra.shu.ac.uk/daol/articles/open/2002/002/antaki2002002-paper.html.

Atkinson, J. M., & Heritage, J. C. (Eds.). (1984). *Structures of social action: Studies in conversational analysis.* Cambridge: Cambridge University Press.

Atkinson, P., & Silverman, D. (1997). Kundera's immortality: The interview society and the invention of the self. *Qualitative Inquiry, 3*(3), 304–325.

Attride-Stirling, J. (2001). Thematic networks: An analytic tool for qualitative research. *Qualitative Research, 1*(3), 385–405.

Banglastories. (n.d.). *Interviewing your own family.* LSE/Runnymede Trust. [Online]. Retrieved May 5, 2020, from http://www.banglastories.org/about-the-project/interviewing-your-own-family.html.

Barad, K. (2007). *Meeting the universe halfway: Quantum physics and the entanglement of matter and meaning.* Durham: Duke University Press.

Barkhuizen, G. (2011). Narrative knowledging in TESOL. *TESOL Quarterly, 45*(3), 391–414.

Barthes, R. (1966/1977). Introduction to the structural analysis of narratives. In R. Barthes (Ed.), *Image-music-text* (S. Heath, Trans.). Glasgow: Collins.

Bartlett, J. G., Iwasaki, Y., Gottlieb, B., Hall, D., & Mannell, R. (2007). Framework for aboriginal-guided decolonizing research involving Métis and First Nations persons with diabetes. *Social Science & Medicine, 65*, 2371–2382.

BBC. (2019). *Academy: Journalism/Skills/Interviewing.* [Online]. Retrieved May 5, 2020, from https://www.bbc.co.uk/academy/en.

BBC Radio 4. (n.d.). *The Listening Project.* [Online]. Retrieved July 21, 2019, from http://www.bbc.co.uk/programmes/b01cqx3b.

Billig, M. (1999a). Whose terms? Whose ordinariness? Rhetoric and ideology in Conversation Analysis. *Discourse and Society, 10*(4), 543–558.

Billig, M. (1999b). Conversation Analysis and the claims of naivety. *Discourse and Society, 10*(4), 572–576.

Blommaert, J. (2001). Investigating narrative inequality: African asylum seekers' stories in Belgium. *Discourse & Society, 12*(4), 413–449.

Bloomberg, L. D., & Volpe, M. (2008). *Completing your qualitative dissertation: A roadmap from beginning to end.* Los Angeles: Sage.

Bolden, G. B. (2009). Implementing incipient actions: The discourse marker 'so' in English conversation. *Journal of Pragmatics, 41*(5), 974–998.

Boyatzis, R. E. (1998). *Transforming qualitative information: Thematic analysis and code development.* London: Sage.

Braun, V., & Clarke, V. (2006). Using thematic analysis in psychology. *Qualitative Research in Psychology, 3*(2), 77–101.

Braun, V., & Clarke, V. (2019). Reflecting on reflexive thematic analysis. *Qualitative Research in Sport, Exercise and Health, 11*(4), 589–597.

Briggs, C. (1986). *Learning how to ask: A sociolinguistic appraisal of the role of the interview in social science research.* Cambridge: Cambridge University Press.

Briggs, C. (2007). Anthropology, interviewing, and communicability in contemporary society. *Current Anthropology, 48*(4), 555–580.

Brinkmann, S. (2018). The interview. In N. K. Denzin & Y. S. Lincoln (Eds.), *The Sage handbook of qualitative research* (pp. 576–599). SAGE: Los Angeles.

Brinkmann, S., & Kvale, S. (2015). *InterViews: Learning the craft of qualitative research interviewing* (3rd ed.). Los Angeles: Sage.

British Association for Applied Linguistics. (2006). *Recommendations on good practice in applied linguistics.* [Online]. Retrieved February 5, 2019, from www.baal.org.uk/dox/goodpractice_full.pdf.

Brumfit, C. J. (1995). Teacher professionalism and research. In G. Cook & B. Seidlhofer (Eds.), *Principle and practice in applied linguistics.* Oxford: Oxford University Press.

Cameron, D., Frazer, E., Harvey, P., Rampton, M. B. H., & Richardson, K. (1992). *Researching language: Issues of power and method.* New York: Routledge.

Census 2011 Results. [Online]. Retrieved April 18, 2014, from http://www.york.gov.uk/info/200630/census/249/census/2.

Centre for Global Education York. (2014a). [Online]. Retrieved July 2, 2019, from https://www.theCentreforGlobalEducationYorkork.org.

Centre for Global Education York. (2014b). *The Hidden Stories of York Project Evaluation.* [Online]. Retrieved July 10, 2016, from www.centreforglobaleducation.org/projects-widening-circle.html.

Cicourel, A. V. (1964). *Method and measurement in sociology.* New York: Free Press.

Clark, H. H., & Schober, M. F. (1992). Asking questions and influencing answers. In J. M. Tanur (Ed.), *Questions about questions* (pp. 15–48). New York: Russell Sage Foundation.

Clayman, S. E., & Heritage, J. (2002). *The news interview: Journalists and public figures on the air.* Cambridge: Cambridge University Press.

Clough, P., & Nutbrown, C. (2012). *A student's guide to methodology* (3rd ed.). London: Sage.

Cotton, K. (1988). *Classroom questioning.* Northwest Regional Educational Laboratory.

Coulmas, F. (Ed.). (1986). *Direct and indirect speech.* Berlin: Mouton dc Gruyter'.

Craig, G., Adamson, S., Ali, N., & Demsash, F. (2010). *Mapping rapidly changing minority ethnic populations: A case study of York.* Joseph Rowntree Foundation. [Online]. Retrieved March 20, 2019, from www.jrf.org.uk/publications/changing-minority-ethnic-populations.

Creese, A. (2008). Linguistic ethnography. In K. A. King & N. H. Hornberger (Eds.), *Encyclopedia of language and education, volume 10: Research methods in language and education* (2nd ed., pp. 229–241). New York: Springer Science and Business Media LLC.

Cruz, M. P. (2009). Towards an alternative relevance-theoretic approach to interjections. *International Review of Pragmatics, 1*(1), 182–206.

Czarniawska, B. (2004). *Narratives in social science research.* London: Sage.

Data Protection Act. (1998).

Davies, B., & Harré, R. (1991). Positioning: The discursive production of selves. *Journal for the Theory of Social Behaviour, 20*(1), 43–63.

De Fina, A., & Georgakopoulou, A. (2008). Analysing narratives as practices. *Qualitative Research, 8*(3), 379–387.

De Fina, A., & Georgakopoulou, A. (2011). *Analysing narrative: Discourse and sociolinguistic perspectives.* Cambridge: Cambridge University Press.

De Fina, A., & Perrino, S. (2011). Introduction: Interviews vs. 'natural' contexts: A false dilemma. *Language in Society, 40*(1), 1–11.

Denzin, N. K., & Lincoln, Y. S. (2011). *The Sage handbook of qualitative research.* Thousand Oaks: Sage.

Drew, P., & Heritage, J. (Eds.) (1992). *Talk at work: Interaction in institutional settings.* Cambridge: Cambridge University Press.

Duranti, A. (1997). *Linguistic anthropology*. Cambridge: Cambridge University Press.

Duranti, A. (2011). 3 - Linguistic anthropology: The study of language as a non-neutral medium. In R. Mesthrie (Ed.), *The Cambridge handbook of sociolinguistics*. Cambridge: Cambridge University Press.

Edmondson, W., & House, J. (1991). Do learners talk too much? The waffle phenomenon in interlanguage pragmatics. In R. Phillipson, E. Kellerman, L. Selinker, M. Sharwood-Smith, & M. Swain (Eds.), *Foreign/second language pedagogy research*. Clevedon: Multilingual Matters.

Edwards, D. (2003). Analyzing racial discourse: The discursive psychology of mind-world relationships. In H. van den Berg, M. Wetherell, & H. Houtkoop-Steenstra (Eds.), *Analyzing race talk: Multidisciplinary approaches to the interview*. Cambridge: Cambridge University Press.

Fairclough, N., & Wodak, R. (1997). Critical discourse analysis. In T. Van Dijk (Ed.), *Discourse studies: A multidisciplinary introduction*. London: Sage.

Fetterman, D. M. (2010). *Ethnography: Step-by-step* (3rd ed.). London: Sage.

Firth, A. (1990). Lingua franca negotiations: Towards an interactional approach. *World Englishes, 9*(3), 269–280.

Fox Tree, J. E., & Schrock, J. C. (2002). Basic meanings of you know and I mean. *Journal of Pragmatics, 34*(6), 727–747.

Freedom of Information Act. (2000). [Online]. Retrieved February 1, 2019, from www.legislation.gov.uk/ukpga/2000/36/pdfs/ukpga_20000036_en.pdf.

Gardner, R. (2001). *When listeners talk: Response tokens and listener stance*. Amsterdam; Philadelphia: John Benjamins Publishing Company.

Gardner, R. (2004). On delaying the answer: Question sequences extended after the question. In R. Gardner & J. Wagner (Eds.), *Second language conversations*. London: Continuum.

Garfinkel, H. (1967). *Studies in ethnomethodology*. Englewood Cliffs, NJ: Prentice Hall.

Garton, S., & Copland, F. (2010). 'I like this interview; I get cakes and cats!': The effect of prior relationships on interview talk. *Qualitative Research, 10*(5), 533–551.

Gee, J. P. (2005). *An introduction to discourse analysis: Theory and method*. Abingdon: Routledge.

Gibbs, G. R. (2007). Thematic coding and categorizing. In *Analyzing qualitative data*. London: Sage.

Gilboy, R., & Zobel, J. (2014). *The hidden stories of York (2013–2014) report*. [Online]. Retrieved February 10, 2019, from www.centreforglobaleducation.org/documents/HiddenStoriesofYorkprojectdetailsMay2014.pdf.

Glaser, B. G., & Strauss, A. L. (1967). *The discovery of grounded theory: Strategies for qualitative research*. Chicago: Aldine.

Goffman, E. (1983). The interaction order. *American Sociological Review, 48*, 1–17.

Greder, A. (2008). *The Island*. Sydney, NSW: Allen and Unwin Children's Books.

Gubrium, J., Holstein, J. A., Marvasti, A. B., & McKinney, A. D. (Eds.). (2012). *The Sage handbook of interviewing: The complexity of the craft*. Thousand Oaks: Sage.

Gumperz, J. (1982). *Discourse strategies*. Cambridge: Cambridge University Press.

Hak, T. (2003). Interviewer laughter as an unspecified request for clarification. In H. van de Berg, M. Wergerell, & H. Houtkoop-Steenstara (Eds.), *Analysing race talk: Multidisciplinary approaches to the interview*. Cambridge: Cambridge University Press.

Hall, C. J., & Wicaksono, R. (2020). Approaching ontologies of English. In C. J. Hall & R. Wicaksono (Eds.), *Ontologies of English: Conceptualising the language for learning, teaching, and assessment* (pp. 3–12). Cambridge: Cambridge University Press.

Hall, C. J., Wicaksono, R., Liu, S., Qian, Y., & Xu, X. (2015). Exploring teachers' ontologies of English: Monolithic conceptions of grammar in a group of Chinese teachers. *International Journal of Applied Linguistics, 27*, 87–109.

Hall, C. J., Smith, P. H., & Wicaksono, R. (2017). *Mapping applied linguistics: An introduction for students and practitioners*. Abingdon: Routledge.

Hammersley, M., & Atkinson, P. (2019). *Ethnography: Principles in practice*. Abingdon: Routledge.

ten Have, P. (1990). *Methodological issues in conversation analysis*. [Online]. Retrieved January 28, 2020, from www.paultenhave.nl/mica.htm.

ten Have, P. (1991). Talk and institution: A reconsideration of the 'asymmetry' of doctor-patient interaction. In D. Boden & D. H. Zimmerman (Eds.), *Talk and social structure: Studies in ethnomethodology and conversation analysis*. Cambridge: Polity Press.

ten Have, P. (2007). *Doing conversation analysis: A practical guide*. London: Sage.

Heritage, J. (1984). A change-of-state-token end aspects of its sequential placement. In J. M. Atkinson & J. Heritage (Eds.), *Structures of social action: Studies in conversation analysis* (pp. 299–345). Cambridge, UK: Cambridge University Press.

Heritage, J. (2010). Questioning in medicine. In A. Freed & S. Ehrlich (Eds.), *Why do you ask?: The function of questions in institutional discourse*. New York: Oxford University Press.

Heritage, J., & Robinson, J. D. (2011). Some versus any medical issues: Encouraging patients to reveal their unmet concerns. In C. Antaki (Ed.), *Applied conversation analysis: Intervention and change in institutional talk*. Basingstoke: Palgrave.

Heritage, J. C., & Watson, D. R. (1979). Formulations as conversational objects. In G. Psathas (Ed.), *Everyday language: Studies in ethnomethodology*. New York: Irvington.

Historypin. (n.d.). [Online]. Retrieved May 5, 2020, from www.historypin.org/project/44-all-our-stories.

Hollway, W. (2005). Commentary. *Qualitative Research in Psychology, 2*, 312–314.

Holmes, J., & Marra, M. (2011). Harnessing storytelling as a sociopragmatic skill: Applying narrative research to workplace English courses. *TESOL Quarterly, 45*(3), 510–534.

Holstein, J. A., & Gubrium, J. F. (1995). Qualitative research methods, Vol. 37. *The active interview*. Thousand Oaks: Sage.

Holstein, J. A., & Gubrium, J. F. (2000). *The self we live by: Narrative identity in a postmodern world*. Oxford: Oxford University Press.

Holstein, J. A., & Gubrium, J. F. (2004). The active interview. In D. Silverman (Ed.), *Qualitative research: Theory, method and practice* (2nd ed.). London: Sage.

Holt, E. (1996). Reporting on talk: The use of direct reported speech in conversation. *Research on Language and Social Interaction, 29*(3), 219–245.

Holt, E. (2017). Indirect reported speech in storytelling: Its position, design, and uses. *Research on Language and Social Interaction, 50*(2), 171–187.

Hughes, J., & Sherrock, W. (1997). *The philosophy of social research*. London: Pearson Longman.

Humans of Bombay. (2020). [Instagram]. Retrieved May 5, 2020, from https://www.instagram.com/officialhumansofbombay/?hl=en.

Humans of Fashion. (2020). [Instagram]. Retrieved May 5, 2020, from https://www.instagram.com/humansoffashionf/?hl=en.

Humans of Leeds. (2020). [Instagram]. Retrieved May 5, 2020, from https://www.instagram.com/humansofleeds/?hl=en.

Humans of New York. (n.d.). [Online]. Retrieved May 5, 2020, from www.humansofnewyork.com.

Humans of University. (2020). [Instagram]. Retrieved May 5, from https://www.instagram.com/humansofuniversity/?hl=en.

Hymes, D. H. (Ed.). (1964). *Language in culture and society: A reader in linguistics and anthropology*. New York: Harper & Row.

Hymes, D. (1968). The ethnography of speaking. In J. Fishman (Ed.), *Readings in the sociology of language* (pp. 99–138). The Hague: Moulton.

Hymes, D. (2010). A perspective for linguistic anthropology. *Journal of Sociolinguistics, 14*(5), 569–580.

Jefferson, G. (2004). Glossary of transcript symbols with an introduction. In G. H. Lerner (Ed.), *Conversation analysis: Studies from the first generation*. Amsterdam; Philadelphia: John Benjamins Publishing Company.

Jefferson, G., Sacks, H., & Schegloff, E. A. (1987). Notes on laugher in the pursuit of intimacy. In G. Button & J. R. E. Lee (Eds.), *Talk and social organisation* (pp. 152–205). Clevedon: Multilingual Matters.

KALW. (2014). *Hear Here*. [Online]. Retrieved May 5, 2020, from www.kalw.org/topic/hear-here.

Kitzinger, C. (2011). Working with childbirth helplines: The contributions and limitations of conversation analysis. In C. Antaki (Ed.), *Applied conversation analysis: Intervention and change in institutional talk* (pp. 98–118). Basingstoke: Palgrave Macmillan.

Kvale, S. (2007). *Doing interviews.* London: Sage.

Labov, W., & Waletzky, J. (1967). Narrative analysis: Oral versions of Personal Experience. In J. Helm (Ed.), *Essays on the verbal and visual arts* (pp. 12–44). Seattle: University of Washington.

Lee, D. A. (2003). Constructivist processes in discourse: A cognitive linguistics perspective. In H. van den Berg, M. Wetherell, & H. Houtkoop-Steenstra (Eds.), *Analyzing race talk.* Cambridge: Cambridge University Press.

Linguistic Ethnography Forum. (2014). [Online]. Retrieved July 11, 2019, from http://www.uklef.net.

Lobley, L. (2001). Whose personality is it anyway? The production of 'Personality' in a diagnostic interview. In A. McHoul & M. Rapley (Eds.), *How to analyse talk in institutional settings.* London: Continuum.

Mann, S. (2008). A reflective approach to qualitative interviewing. Paper delivered at *Advances in Ethnography, Language and Communication,* Aston University.

Mann, S. (2011). A critical review of qualitative interviews in applied linguistics. *Applied Linguistics, 32*(1), 6–24.

Mann, S. (2016). *The research interview: Reflective practice and reflexivity in research processes.* Basingstoke: Palgrave Macmillan.

Marn, T., & Wolgemuth, J. R. (2017). Purposeful entanglements: A new materialist analysis of transformative interviews. *Qualitative Inquiry, 23*(5), 365–374.

Maybin, J., & Tusting, K. (2011). Linguistic ethnography. In J. Simpson (Ed.), *The Routledge handbook of applied linguistics.* London: Routledge.

Mazeland, H., & ten Have, P. (1996). Essential tensions in (semi-) open research interviews. In I. Maso & D. Wester (Eds.), *The deliberate dialogue: Qualitative perspectives on the interview.* Brussels: VUB University Press.

Menard-Warwick, J. (2011). A methodological reflection on the process of narrative analysis: Alienation and identity in the life histories of English language teachers. *TESOL Quarterly, 45*(3), 564–574.

Merrill, B., & West, L. (2009). *Using biographical methods in social research.* London: Sage.

O'Keeffe, A., & Walsh, S. (2012). Applying corpus linguistics and conversation analysis in the investigation of small group teaching in Higher Education. *Corpus Linguistics and Linguistic Theory, 8*(1), 159–181.

Oral History Project: Giving Voice to the American Latino Experience. (2015). *'Learn to Interview', 'How to Video' and 'How to Kit'.* University of Texas Libraries: University of Texas, Austin, USA. [Online]. Retrieved September 19, 2019, from http://www.lib.utexas.edu/voces/training-index.html.

Pavlenko, A. (2007). Autobiographic narratives as data in applied linguistics. *Applied Linguistics, 28*(2), 163–188.

Peters, P., & Wong, D. (2015). Turn management and backchannels. In K. Aijmer & C. Rühlemann (Eds.), *Corpus pragmatics: A handbook* (pp. 408–429). Cambridge: Cambridge University Press.

Poland, B. (1995). Transcription quality as an aspect of rigor in qualitative research. *Qualitative Inquiry, 1*(3), 290–310.

Pomerantz, A. (1986). Extreme case formulations: A way of legitimizing claims. *Human Studies, 9*(2/3), 219–229.

Pomerantz, A., & Zemel, A. (2003). Perspectives and frameworks in interviewers' queries. In H. van de Berg, M. Wertherell, & H. Houtkoop-Steenstara (Eds.), *Analysing race talk: Multidisciplinary approaches to the interview.* Cambridge: Cambridge University Press.

Potter, J., & Hepburn, A. (2005). Qualitative interviews in psychology: Problems and possibilities. *Qualitative Research in Psychology, 2*(4), 281–307.

Potter, J., & Hepburn, A. (2012). Eight challenges for interview researchers. In J. F. Gubrium, J. A. Holstein, A. Marvasti, & K. McKinney (Eds.), *The Sage handbook of interview research: The complexity of the craft* (pp. 555–570). Los Angeles: Sage.

Psathas, G. (1995). *Conversation analysis: The study of talk-in-interaction.* Thousand Oaks: Sage.

Puchta, C., & Potter, J. (1999). Asking elaborate questions: Focus groups and the management of spontaneity. *Journal of Sociolinguistics, 3*, 314–335.

Rampton, B., Tusting, K., Maybin, J., Barwell, R., Creese, A., & Lytra, V. (2004). *UK linguistic ethnography: A discussion paper.* Unpublished. [Online]. Retrieved August 10, 2019, from www.ling-ethnog.org.uk.

Rapley, T. J. (2001). The art(fulness) of open-ended interviewing: Some considerations on analysing interviews. *Qualitative Research, 1*(3), 303–323.

Rapley, T. (2012). The (extra)ordinary practices of qualitative interviewing. In J. F. Gubrium, J. A. Holstein, A. Marvasti, & K. McKinney (Eds.), *The Sage handbook of interview research: The complexity of the craft.* Los Angeles, CA: Sage.

Rapley, T. (2019). The way(s) of interviewing. Exploring social studies of interviews. In K. Roulston (Ed.), *Interactional studies of qualitative research interviews* (pp. 271–282). Amsterdam; Philadelphia: John Benjamins Publishing Company.

Richards, K. (2005). Introduction. In K. Richards & P. Seedhouse (Eds.), *Applying conversation analysis.* Basingstoke: Palgrave Macmillan.

Richards, K. (2011). Using micro-analysis in interviewer training: 'Continuers' and interviewer positioning. *Applied Linguistics, 32*(1), 95–112.

Roberts, C., Davies, E., & Jupp, T. (1992). *Language and discrimination: A study of communication in multi-ethnic workplaces.* Harlow, UK: Longman.

Robson, C. (2011). *Real world research: A resource for users of social research methods in applied settings*. Chichester, UK: Wiley.

Rodger, R., & Herbert, J. (Eds.). (2007). *Testimonies of the city: Identity, community and change in a contemporary urban world*. Aldershot: Ashgate Publishing.

Rodger, R., & Herbert, J. (2008). Narratives of South Asian women in Leicester 1964–2004. *Oral History, 36*(2), 554–563.

Roulston, K. (2001). Data analysis and 'theorising as ideology'. *Qualitative Research, 1*(3), 279–302.

Roulston, K. (2006). Close encounters of the 'CA' kind: A review of literature analysing talk in research interviews. *Qualitative Research, 6*(4), 515–534.

Roulston, K. (2010). *Reflective interviewing: A guide to theory and practice*. London: Sage.

Roulston, K. (2011). Interview 'problems' as topics for analysis. *Applied Linguistics, 32*(1), 77–94.

Roulston, K. (2014). Interactional problems in research interviews. *Qualitative Research, 14*(3), 227–293.

Roulston, K. J., Baker, C. D., & Liljestrom, A. (2001). Analyzing the researcher's work in generating data: The case of complaints. *Qualitative Inquiry, 7*(6), 745–772.

Rowe, M. B. (1987). Wait-time: Slowing down may be a way of speeding up. *American Educator, 11*(47), 38–43.

Rubin, H. J., & Rubin, I. S. (2012). *Qualitative interviewing: The art of hearing data* (3rd ed.). Los Angeles: Sage.

Sacks, H. (1984). Notes on methodology. In J. M. Atkinson & J. Heritage (Eds.), *Structures of social action* (pp. 21–27). Cambridge: Cambridge University Press.

Sacks, H., Schegloff, E., & Jefferson, G. (1974). A simplest systematics for the organization of turn taking for conversation. *Language, 50*, 696–735.

Schegloff, E. A. (1982). Discourse as an interactional achievement: Some uses of 'uh huh' and other things that come between sentences. In D. Tannen (Ed.), *Analyzing discourse: Text and talk* (pp. 71–93). Washington, DC: Georgetown University Press.

Schegloff, E. A. (1991). Reflecting on talk and social structure. In D. Boden & D. Zimmerman (Eds.), *Talk and social structure*. Cambridge: Polity.

Schegloff, E. A. (1999a). Schegloff's texts' as Billig's data: A critical reply. *Discourse and Society, 10*(4), 558–572.

Schegloff, E. A. (1999b). Naivete vs sophistication or discipline vs self-indulgence: A rejoinder to Billig. *Discourse and Society, 10*(4), 577–582.

Schegloff, E. A. (2007). *Sequence organization in interaction: A primer in conversation analysis volume 1*. Cambridge: Cambridge University Press.

Schiffrin, D. (1987). *Discourse markers*. Cambridge: Cambridge University Press.

Schostak, J. (2006). *Interviewing and representation in qualitative research*. Maidenhead, UK: Open University Press.

Schubert, S. J., Hansen, S., Dyer, K. R., & Rapley, M. (2009). "'ADHD patient" or "illicit drug user"? Managing medico-moral membership categories in drug dependence services. *Discourse and Society, 20*(4), 499–516.

Schuman, H. (1982). Artifacts are in the mind of the beholder. *American Sociologist, 17*(1), 21–28.

Seidman, I. (2012). *Interviewing as qualitative research: A guide for researchers in education and the social sciences* (4th ed.). New York: Teachers College.

Silverman, D. (2004). Foreword. In B. Czarniawska (Ed.), *Narratives in social science research.* London: Sage.

Silverman, D. (Ed.). (2010). *Qualitative research: Theory, method and practice.* London: Sage.

Silverman, D. (2013). *Doing qualitative research: A practical handbook* (4th ed.). London: Sage.

Silverman, D. (2015). *Interpreting qualitative data: Methods for analysing talk, text and interaction* (5th ed.). Thousand Oaks: Sage.

Silverman, D. (2017). How was it for you? The Interview Society and the irresistible rise of the (poorly analyzed) interview. *Qualitative Research, 17*(2), 144–158.

Smith-Khan, L. (2017). Negotiating narratives, accessing asylum: Evaluating language policy as multi-level practice, beliefs and management. *Multilingua, 36*, 31–57.

Stahl, R. J. (1994). Using 'think-time' and 'wait-time' skillfully in the classroom. *ERIC Digest, 6*.

StoryCorps. (n.d.). [Online]. Retrieved July 17, 2019, from https://storycorps.org.

Storying Sheffield Telling Untold Stories. (n.d.). [Online]. Retrieved February 10, 2019, from www.storyingsheffield.com.

Talmy, S. (2010). Qualitative interviews in applied linguistics: From research instrument to social practice. *Annual Review of Applied Linguistics, 30*, 128–148.

Talmy, S. (2011). The interview as collaborative achievement: Interaction, identity and ideology in a speech event. *Applied Linguistics, 32*(1), 25–42.

Talmy, S., & Richards, K. (2010). Theorizing qualitative research interviews in applied linguistics. *Applied Linguistics, 32*(1), 1–5.

Tama, M. C. (1989). Critical thinking: Promoting it in the classroom. *ERIC Digest, 6*.

Teesdale, C. (2016). *Humans of London.* London: LOM Art.

The ALLIANCE. (2019). *Humans of Scotland.* [Online]. Retrieved May 5, 2020, from https://www.alliance-scotland.org.uk/wp-content/uploads/2019/09/HOS-Ebook.pdf.

The East Midlands Oral History Archive. (n.d.). *How do I conduct an oral history interview?* Centre for Urban History, University of Leicester: Leicester. [Online]. Retrieved January 28, 2020, from https://www.le.ac.uk/emoha/training/no2.pdf.

The Office for National Statistics (2014). Migration Statistics Quarterly Report, August 2014 [Online] Available at: www.ons.gov.uk/ons/rel/migration1/migration-statistics-quarterly-report/august-2014/stb-msqr-august-2014.html.

The Oxford English Dictionary. (2014). [Online]. Retrieved August 22, 2019, from www.oed.com.

The Stanford Storytelling Project. (n.d.). [Online]. Retrieved May 5, 2020, from https://storytelling.stanford.edu.

The University of Sheffield. (n.d.). *Researching Community Heritage.* [Online]. Retrieved May 5, 2020, from www.communityheritage.group.shef.ac.uk.

The World Values Survey. (n.d.). [Online]. Retrieved November 20, 2019, from www.worldvaluessurvey.org.

Todorov, T. (1971/77). The poetics of prose. In B. Czarniawska (Ed.). (2004) *Narratives in social science research.* London: Sage.

Toohey, K. (2019). The onto-epistemologies of New Materialism: Implications for applied linguistics pedagogies and research. *Applied Linguistics, 40*(6), 937–956.

Tuckett, A. G. (2005). Applying thematic analysis theory to practice: A researcher's experience. *Contemporary Nurse, 19*(1–2), 75–87.

UK Data Archive. (n.d.). [Online]. Retrieved February 10, 2019, from www.data-archive.ac.uk.

Usher, R. (1996). A critique of the neglected epistemological assumptions of educational research. In D. Scott & R. Usher (Eds.), *Understanding educational research.* London; New York: Routledge.

Van den Berg, H., Wetherell, M., & Houtkoop-Steenstra, H. (Eds.). (2003). *Analyzing race talk: Multidisciplinary approaches to the interview.* Cambridge: Cambridge University Press.

Veterans History Project. (2005). *Sample interview questions for veterans.* American Folklife Center: Library of Congress, USA. [Online]. Retrieved September 10, 2019, from http://www.loc.gov/vets/questions.html.

Wetherell, M. (1998). Positioning and interpretive repertoires: Conversation analysis and post-structuralism in dialogue. *Discourse and Society, 9*(3), 387–412.

Wetherell, M. (2003). Racism and the analysis of cultural resources in interviews. In H. van den Berg, M. Wetherell, & H. Houtkoop-Steenstra (Eds.), *Analyzing race talk: Multidisciplinary approaches to the interview.* Cambridge: Cambridge University Press.

Wicaksono, R. (2012). 'Raising students' awareness of the construction of communicative (in)competence in international classrooms. In J. Ryan (Ed.), *Cross cultural teaching and learning for home and international students: Internationalisation of pedagogy and curriculum in higher education.* London; New York: Routledge.

Wicaksono, R., & Hall, C. J. (2020). Using ontologies of English'. In C. J. Hall & R. Wicaksono (Eds.), *Ontologies of English: Conceptualising the language for learning, teaching, and assessment* (pp. 368–376). Cambridge: Cambridge University Press.

Wicaksono, R., & Zhurauskaya, D. (2011). *Introducing English as a Lingua Franca: An online tutorial.* [Online]. Retrieved June 28, 2016, from www.englishlinguafranca.com.

Wierzbicka, A. (1992). The semantics of interjection. *Journal of Pragmatics, 18*(2–3), 159–192.

Wilkins, D. P. (1992). Interjections as deictics. *Journal of Pragmatics, 18*(2–3), 119–158.

Youzi Project. (n.d.). [Online]. Retrieved February 10, 2019, from www.youziproject.com.

INDEX